Delivering Knock Your Socks Off Service

Kristin Anderson | Ron Zemke

Co-author of
SERVICE AMERICA

amacom

American Management Association

This publication is designed to provide accurate and authoritative
information in regard to the subject matter covered. It is sold with
the understanding that the publisher is not engaged in rendering
legal, accounting, or other professional service. If legal advice or
other expert assistance is required, the services of a competent
professional person should be sought.

Library of Congress Cataloging-in-Publication Data

Anderson, Kristin.
    Delivering knock your socks off service / Kristin Anderson, Ron
Zemke.
        p.   cm.
    ISBN 0-8144-7777-1
    1. Customer service.   I. Zemke, Ron.   II. Title.
HF5415.5.A53   1991
658.8'12—dc20   91-53048
                                                          CIP

DELIVERING KNOCK YOUR SOCKS OFF SERVICE®
is a registered trademark of Performance Research Associates, Inc.

Artwork © John Bush

Printing number

11

Table of Contents

Preface

What You Do Is Critically Important

Expectations are critical when you serve customers. Meet them to satisfy the customer. Exceed them to make the customer love you. Set unrealistic expectations—in essence, promises you can never hope to keep—and your customers will hold you beneath contempt.

—Robert A. Peterson
Researcher, Department of Marketing,
University of Texas, Austin

Serving customers. The two words cover so much. Answering questions. Solving problems. Untangling corporate logjams. Fixing what's broken and finding what's lost. Soothing the irate and reassuring the timid. And time after time, performing the business equivalent of pulling a rabbit out of a hat: Matching people who do business with you with just the right products and services.

Not too long ago, working in customer service was just about as thankless a job as a person could find. Sales? That was a job with a future. Marketing? Now there was a title with some prestige. Advertising? What mystique! But customer service? A drain on the budget. A time-eating burden. A career path to nowhere. Fellow employees looked down their noses at "those people who deal with whining customers." And customers—well, they mostly seemed to see customer service as a title for not very bright people who woke up most mornings, looked in the mirror, grinned wide, and said to their reflections, "This will be a *wonderful* day. I'm going to go down there and tick off the first 217 people I see." And then did just that. Not exactly positive images.

But that was then. And this is now. Beginning in the mid-1980s, professional business watchers began to notice something important, not to mention surprising, on the service front. They discovered that a few organizations that had dedicated themselves to working hard at giving their customers superior service were producing better results. These organizations grew faster (even though a lot of the time they charged more for their basic products and services) and were more profitable than the organizations that were still working as hard as they could to give their customers as little as possible.

▲ In short, companies that emphasized service were starting to make more money than companies that didn't.

Researchers also started to notice that successful service organizations had lower marketing costs, fewer upset and complaining customers, and more repeat business—customers were "voting with their feet" and beating a path back to the doors of the companies that served them well. What's more, good service had internal rewards: Employee turnover and absenteeism were lower and morale and job satisfaction higher in these same organizations.

▲ Organizations that focused on superior customer service turned out to be all-around better, more successful companies than those that treated customers like the enemy and customer service as either a grudging afterthought or a necessary evil.

Almost overnight, being customer focused, understanding and meeting customer needs, coddling customers with tender loving care, and giving quality customer service have become the new, strategically important management concerns. Theories have been developed. Books written. Posters hung. Films made. All across the United States—no, all around the world, really—people are talking about service, service, service.

But for all the hype and hoopla, what it really comes down to is: You. What you do is important. What you do is work—hard work. Answering questions. Solving problems. Untangling corporate logjams. Fixing what's broken and finding what's lost. Soothing the irate and reassuring the timid. And time after time, performing the business equivalent of pulling a rabbit out of a hat: Matching people you do business with with just the right products and services.

The difference between then and now? Today, "they" know what you do is important. The theys in your organization have begun to realize how much they—and, in truth, the whole organization—depend on you doing your job well, thoughtfully, skillfully, and to the customer's delight. More than ever before, they now understand how important it is that you have the time, the tools, the training, the support, and the backing and encouragement to not just satisfy your customers, but to deliver service that's so good it "knocks their socks off," bringing customers back eager and asking for more of the same.

The purpose of this book is to share with you what we have learned about quality customer care over fifteen years of watching and working with thousands of quality-oriented customer service professionals. We're talking about people just like you who provide great service over and over and over again; true Knock Your Socks Off Service pros who make their customers' lives and jobs easier instead of harder, more interesting and less boring—and who have a heck of a good time doing it, too.

What you do is more important to your organization than ever before. If this book helps you do it even a little bit better, thank the thousands of pros who taught us, not us. And if you find the journey through these pages not only helpful, but enjoyable, then we'll have met our service goal.

Kristin Anderson
Ron Zemke

Minneapolis
April 1991

The Fundamental Principles of Knock Your Socks Off Service

Delivering Knock Your Socks Off Service—the kind of service that makes a positive, lasting impression on your customers—takes more than simple courtesy. Much more.

It starts with understanding what good service is from *your customer's* point of view. What you do, how you do it, how well it must be done, and proving you can do it again—those are the fundamentals.

Delivering Knock Your Socks Off Service means creating a memorable experience for every customer. It means meeting expectations and satisfying needs—and in such a way that you're seen as easy to do business with.

The customer who experiences all that will be your customer again and again. When you deliver Knock Your Socks Off Service, everybody wins: your customer, your company, and *you.*

1

The Only Unbreakable Rule:

To the Customer, *You* Are the Company

Customer relations is an integral part of your job—not an extension of it.

—William B. Martin
Quality Customer Service

Customers don't distinguish between you and the company you work for. Nor should they. To your customer's way of thinking, you *are* the company.

Customers don't know how things get done behind doors marked EMPLOYEES ONLY. They don't know your areas of responsibility, your job description, or what you personally can and cannot do for them. And they don't care. To customers, those things are *your* business, not theirs.

▲ The attitude is clear: "Serve me my meal." "Help me with this purchase, please." "Solve my problem." "Take my order, *now.*"

3

Whether customers' feelings about the company are good or bad often relates directly to their experience with you. A few years ago, British Airways, one of Europe's premier air carriers, surveyed its customers to find out what they thought about the airline. The company learned that the skill and attitudes of its people were basic to how customers saw the company. To the customer, British Airways was far more than just airplanes, tickets, seats, and meals. It was "the friendly person who helped me with my baggage" and "the flight attendant who made sure I knew how to make my next connection."

What does all that mean for you? Donald Porter, senior vice-president of British Airways, explains it this way:

> If you're a service person, and you get it wrong at your point in the customer's chain of experience, you are very likely erasing from the customer's mind all the memories of the good treatment he or she may have had up to that moment. But if you get it right, you have a chance to undo all the wrongs that may have happened before the customer got to you.

You can make or break the chain of great service.

Is it fair that the customer sees you as the company? No! It is *not* fair. Especially when there are so many ways that things can get screwed up—and so many of them are definitely not your fault and not under your control. But fair has nothing to do with it. When your job involves serving customers and dealing with the public, how good a job you do with and for them—for the nice and the nasty, the smart and the dumb, the people you'd like to take home to mother, and those you really wish had never been born—determines how successful your company will be.

▲ In short, you are the company.

Being the Company: It's Everything You Do

Some of the things you do to provide Knock Your Socks Off Service are relatively simple and easy, such as choosing your language carefully.

> **TIP:** Use *I* instead of *they* or *we*. To a customer, the company begins and ends with you. Using *I* shows that you understand and accept that: "*I'm* sorry you had to look so long to find the dress department. May *I* help you find anything else?"
>
> Saying "the *policy* is. . . ." or "*they* won't allow. . . ." tells customers you are just a clerk. If that's the way you feel, you won't ever be able to help them—and could easily be replaced by a machine or walked on like so much carpet.

Other actions you take are more complex. Customers expect you to make the organization work for them. They expect you to understand the big picture and to be able to answer their questions, solve their problems, and refer them to just the right people for just the right things.

What your customers want and need is changing constantly. So is your company, and so are you. How can you possibly keep up? Let the following three questions guide your personal-service efforts. Don't just ask them once. Ask them all the time. Use the information they provide to choose actions that will Knock the Socks Off your customers.

1. *What do my customers want from me, and from my company?* Think both about what your customers *need* and what your customers *expect.*
2. *How do support areas—e.g., billing or shipping—work to serve my customers?* Consider your role in making the different areas of your company work in harmony for your customer.
3. *What are the details—little things—that make a big difference in my customers' satisfaction?* Knock Your Socks Off Service is paying attention to what's important in your customer's eyes. Do you know what counts for your customers?

Being the company to your customers is what makes the work you do both challenging and rewarding. In your one-to-one contact with customers, the once vague, impersonal company takes on shape and substance. In your hands is the power to make that contact magical and memorable. In your hands is the power to keep customers coming back.

Your pledge: "Look out customers—I'm gonna knock your socks off!"

2

Know What Knock Your Socks Off Service Is

✗ Customers perceive service in their own unique, idiosyn-
cratic, emotional, irrational, end-of-the-day, and totally
human terms. Perception is all there is!

—Tom Peters
Management guru

Customers are demanding. And they have every right to be.
Today's customers have more options than ever before. If your
organization doesn't offer what they want or need, if you don't
interact with them in a manner that meets or exceeds their
expectations, they will just walk on down the street—or let
their fingers walk through the Yellow Pages—and do business
with one of your competitors.

▲ And if you don't have customers, you don't have a
job!

Researchers consistently find that it costs *five times more*
to attract a new customer than it does to keep one you already
have. But many businesses think only of making the sale

7

instead of developing long-term customer relationships. Even more disturbing, researchers also find that at any given time, as many as *one customer in four* is dissatisfied enough to start doing business with someone else—if he or she can find someone else who promises to do the same thing that you do but in a slightly more satisfying way. That's as many as twenty-five out of every one hundred people your organization does business with.

Most disturbing of all is the finding that *only one* of those twenty-five dissatisfied customers will ever tell you that he or she is dissatisfied. In fact, you've probably noticed from your own experience how rare it is to deal with customers who can do a really good job of telling you what they want. More often, they just expect you to know—and are disappointed when you don't.

That's why companies spend a lot of time and money these days observing customers as they shop, surveying them by mail, talking to them on the phone, and meeting them face-to-face. Like miners working a claim for the gold they know is there, today's businesses collect and sort customer letters and comment cards, looking for the complaints and the compliments that provide clues about what people want today—and how their needs may change tomorrow.

As a customer service professional, you frequently draw on the knowledge your company has acquired about customers. But you have another, equally important source of information: your own day-to-day contact with your customers. From personal experience, you know quite a lot about what your customers want: which actions meet their expectations, which exceed them—and which disappoint them.

That's your own special edge, the foundation on which to build your own unique way of providing Knock Your Socks Off Service.

Getting Yourself Organized

It's helpful to have a framework to hold together the things you know personally and the information passed on to you by your organization. The framework we like a lot was invented by Texas A&M researcher Dr. Leonard Berry. He and his colleagues observe that customers evaluate service quality on five factors:

1. *Reliability.* The ability to provide what was promised, dependably and accurately.
2. *Responsiveness.* The willingness to help customers promptly.
3. *Assurance.* The knowledge and courtesy you show to customers, and your ability to convey trust, competence, and confidence.
4. *Empathy.* The degree of caring and individual attention you show customers.
5. *Tangibles.* The physical facilities and equipment, and your own (and others') appearance.

Chances are, almost everything you do to and for your customers falls into one of these categories. Consider these common examples:

- When you fulfill a customer order on time, you show *reliability.*
- When you notice a customer puzzling over a product and offer help and information, you show *responsiveness.*
- When you smile and tell a customer, "I can help you with that"—and do—you build *assurance.*
- When you are sensitive to an individual customer's needs when solving a problem, you show *empathy.*
- And when you take the time to make yourself and your work area presentable, you are paying attention to the *tangibles.*

TIP: Using your own knowledge and experience, organize what you know about your customers by making notes on what they expect of you and your organization in each of the five categories. Make a point of adding to and refining this list every day. Think of it as your own personal database.

All five factors are important to your customers. In the next five chapters, let's look at each of these pieces of the customer service puzzle in more detail to see how they combine to create people-pleasing Knock Your Socks Off Service.

> Customer expectations of service organizations are loud and clear: look good, be responsive, be reassuring through courtesy and competence, be empathetic but, most of all, be reliable. Do what you said you would do. Keep the service promise.
>
> —Dr. Leonard Berry
> Researcher, Texas A&M University

3

Knock Your Socks Off Service Is:

Reliable

Undertake not what you cannot perform but be careful to keep your promise.

—George Washington

As commander-in-chief of the Continental forces in the American Revolution, the lives of thousands of men and the fate of an emerging nation rested on George Washington's ability to know what could and could not be accomplished. He had to deliver on his commitments. There was no room for misjudging the situation.

As a service professional, you are part of another kind of revolution: the service revolution. And while lives are seldom on the line, a little piece of the future of your company is—every time you face a customer. That's where reliability comes in.

Service Promises

Reliability means keeping the service promise—doing what you say you will do to and for the customer. Service promises come from a variety of sources:

• *Personal promises:* The majority of customer service promises come from you. These are the promises you make when you tell a customer, "I'll get right back to you with that information," or "You should expect to receive that package in two weeks," or "I understand the problem you are having with your computer, and this software support disk will solve it."

• *Organizational promises:* Promises are made by your organization, both directly and indirectly. Direct promises can be contained in advertising and marketing materials, made in company correspondence and contracts, or published in service guarantees and policies for everyone to see. Indirect promises often are just taken for granted.

For example, McDonald's doesn't advertise that the hamburger you buy in Minneapolis will taste like the hamburger you buy in New York or Seattle or even Japan. But if each McDonald's could arbitrarily change the recipe, the service promise indirectly made by the McDonald's name would clearly be broken, no matter how good any individual recipe might turn out to be.

• *Expected promises:* Your customers bring expectations with them to every service transaction. Based on their past experiences with you and with other service providers, customers make assumptions about what you will and won't do for them. Failing to meet a customer expectation, whether you knew about it or not, even whether you helped to shape it or not, has the same impact as breaking any other promise.

The good news is that as a service professional, you already know many of your customer's expectations. By asking questions and really listening, you will be able to discover others. Promises, whatever their sources, are too important for you to rely on guesswork.

Managing Promises

Promises can and should be managed. Once you know what your customers do and don't expect—the promises they expect you to keep—you are in a position to shape your customer's expectations to match what you can do for them. When you do that well, your customer perceives that your services are reliable.

Let's say you are a salesperson in a custom furniture store. Jane Dowe comes in looking for a desk and credenza, expecting that she can take her purchase with her immediately. She doesn't know that your stock is all custom-built. Your challenge is to change her expectations to match what your organization can do for her:

> "Our custom-crafted desks are of the highest quality.
> I can have the desk you choose today delivered to
> you in two weeks."

Jane may decide that the wait is worth it because of the quality involved. If she really needs the desk today—in which case, you can't change her expectations *this* time—at least she will leave your store knowing that you are honest and concerned with her satisfaction. And she may recommend you to a friend or colleague based on her revised understanding of your capabilities.

Fixing Promises When They Break

Sometimes promises made in good faith can't be kept. As much as we strive to be error-free, it's inevitable that problems will occur. Not everything that affects your customer's experience with you is within your control. What should you do when promises are broken? When you discover a broken promise, or have one pointed out to you, the first thing to do is to apologize. Don't waste time scapegoating—blaming yourself, your company, or your customer. Admit that something has gone wrong, and then immediately find out what your customer needs now. Has the broken promise created another problem? Or has it, perhaps, created an opportunity for you to rescue your reputation for reliability?

For example, suppose Jane had agreed to wait two weeks, but now you've found out that deliveries are running about three days behind schedule. If you don't call with the bad news, you can bet she'll call you when the desk doesn't arrive on the day she was told to expect it—and she won't be happy about the delay. On the other hand, if you take the initiative, you might discover that the delay is acceptable. Or, if she has an important meeting and needs furniture in her office on that specific day, you can arrange for a loaner until the order arrives. Then, you (and your company) look like a hero.

> **TIP:** Never overpromise just to get the sale. In today's service economy, service doesn't end with the sale, it just begins. Keeping the promises you make and only making promises you can keep is what reliability is all about.

> You can't promise your customers sunny weather, but you can promise to hold an umbrella over them when it rains.
>
> —Sign in a telephone service center

4

Knock Your Socks Off Service Is:

Responsive

A rose on time is far more valuable than a $1,000 gift that's too late.

—Jim Rohn
Author and motivational speaker

Timeliness has always been important. And today, responsive action—doing things in a timely fashion—is even more crucial. Just look around at the number of businesses that have been created to get things done quickly:

- Federal Express won international success by delivering things ABSOLUTELY, POSITIVELY, OVERNIGHT.
- LensCrafters optical stores promise CUSTOM-CRAFTED EYEGLASSES IN ABOUT AN HOUR.
- Domino's became America's largest pizza company by meeting its 30-MINUTE OR $3.00 OFF guarantee.

The big-name national service leaders don't have a corner on the timeliness market. All over town, you can find same-day dry cleaning, fifty-five-minute photo developing, and twenty-four-hour automated banking services. At the same time, a growing number of traditional manufacturing companies are practicing Just-In-Time (JIT) management, ordering things to arrive just in time. Sometimes "just in the nick of time."

Companies that cater to time-conscious customers are everywhere you look. And their success affects your customers' expectations of your willingness and ability to do the same. Small wonder that your customers may be demanding tighter deadlines and faster service than ever before. When they do, they expect you to be responsive.

Setting—and Meeting—Deadlines

Sometimes it seems that everybody wants everything done at the same time. But it's a mistake to think your customers will be unhappy with anything less than "right this instant," just as it's wrong to assume that if you don't tell the customer when a thing will be done, the customer will demand: "Do it yesterday!"

Deadlines are important. But deadlines are created. When you say to a customer, "I'll have it ready for you this afternoon," or, "I'll put it in the mail today," you are creating an expectation for your customer and setting a deadline for yourself. Be realistic, because once created, deadlines become yardsticks by which your customer will measure your success or failure. Knock Your Socks Off Service results from creating acceptable, realistic expectations of responsiveness for your customers, and then meeting those expectations.

As a service professional, you set the tone and agenda. Start by finding out what the customer really needs. There's a big difference between, "I have to have this dry-cleaned to wear next week" and, "I want to have these winter coats cleaned before I put them away for the season." Use that information to pick a time that works well for you and try it out on the customer. Nine times out of ten, you'll hear yes. And if your suggestion doesn't work, your customer will let you know and you can work together to find an alternative—

evidence of responsiveness that customers appreciate and remember.

> **TIP:** The next time you're in doubt, ask your customers, "When would you like this?" You may be pleasantly surprised when they pick a reasonable time, or even ask you, "Well, when could you have it done?" An added benefit is that it gives them a sense of control and involvement. We are all more comfortable when we feel we have some control over our lives and the things that go on around us.

When Customers Must Wait

The best time for anything is the time that is best for the customer. But dissatisfaction isn't measured in minutes. Rather, dissatisfaction is often the result of uncertainty. Research shows that the most frustrating aspect of waiting is *not knowing how long the wait will be.*

Be aware of what your customers think is an appropriate wait. According to a study by *Restaurants & Institutions* magazine, for example, "fast" for fast-food customers means five minutes or less, while diners in a family restaurant expect to

wait as long as thirty minutes for their food to arrive. Similarly, in the retail business, expectations may vary with the time of day or season of the year. Customers are less able, let alone less willing, to wait during their lunch hour than on a lazy Sunday afternoon, and certainly the Christmas shopping season has its own pace compared to other times of the year.

Think about your own experiences as a customer. When you are behind someone who insists on paying off the national debt in pennies or are waiting for the manufacturer to plant and grow the oak trees to make your new furniture, it is the uncertainty—Will I be served sometime this century?—more than the wait itself that gets your blood pumping. As a service professional, you may not be able to count pennies any faster or make trees grow overnight, but you can make waiting less traumatic. Acknowledge waiting customers and keep them informed about what is happening. Be as specific as you can: "I'm with another customer right now, but should be free in about fifteen minutes. If you would like to look around some more, I'll come find you the minute I'm through."

> **TIP:** Pay special attention to waiting time when your customers are out of your sight, whether on the phone, in another part of town, or in another state, rather than standing right in front of you.

In face-to-face settings, acknowledgment doesn't have to be verbal. Bahman Djahanguri, owner of *Yvette*, a formal-dining restaurant in Minneapolis, tells his people, "The eyes are important. Watch all the time. Make eye contact with the customers. Make your actions say, 'I know you are there. I'll be with you very soon.'"

> Time is the scarcest resource, and unless it is managed, nothing else can be managed.
>
> —Peter Drucker
> Management theorist

5

Knock Your Socks Off Service Is:

Reassuring

Consistent, high-quality service boils down to two equally important things: caring and competence.

—Chip R. Bell and Ron Zemke
Service Wisdom

In many companies, the need to improve service quality has given birth to countless hours of "smile training," as though the key to satisfying every customer's needs and expectations involved nothing more than a cheery greeting and a happy-face sticker. Today's customer service professionals know there's much more involved in taking care of business.

If being nice were the answer, good service would be the norm, but that's clearly not the case. Make no mistake: Courtesy, good manners, and civility are important—treat your customers like mud and they'll fling it back at you, every time. But courtesy is not a substitute for competence.

When you provide Knock Your Socks Off Service, your actions assure customers that they are doing business with a well-trained, skillful service professional. Customers know they can trust you because of the competence and confidence you display in your work.

Today, customers expect to be reassured by the people they deal with. And that takes more than mastery of a few simple "people skills." It's the combination of both style and substance that wins accolades and brings customers back again and again.

Bad Service Drives Customers Away

Knock Your Socks Off Service professionals know that inept service has profound consequences. One study on retailing reports that customers identify "salespeople who know less about their products than I do" as a leading reason for switching from department store to catalog shopping. Another study, on the automobile industry, finds that two out of three car buyers refuse to return to the same dealership for their next car. Their reasons have little to do with the car itself and more with the games on the showroom floor and the boorish treatment they encountered when they brought the family chariot in for service that made them determined to look elsewhere.

This is why providing Knock Your Socks Off Service has

such a positive impact on your company, on your customer, and on your career. Good service providers stand out, so make yourself memorable. Combine substance and style—what you do and how you do it—to reassure your customers that you really do know, and care about, what you're doing.

Winning Points on Substance

Knock Your Socks Off Service is built on knowledge and know-how. The substance that backs up your style comes in four packages:

1. *Product Knowledge.* Customers expect you to know the features, advantages, and benefits of whatever it is your company makes, does, or delivers. The salesperson who has to read the manual in front of the customer just to figure out how to turn on the stereo doesn't create an impression of competence.
2. *Company Knowledge.* Customers expect you to know more than the limits of your particular job. They expect you to know how your organization works so you can guide them to someone who can meet their needs if they should fall outside your area of responsibility. Can you help your customer navigate the briar patch that is your business easily and successfully?
3. *Listening Skills.* Customers expect you to listen, understand, and respond to their specific needs as they explain them to you. They expect you to ask pertinent questions that help them do a better job of giving you the information you need to work for them effectively. And they expect you to pay attention and get it right so they don't have to repeat it.
4. *Problem-Solving Skills.* Customers expect that you will be able to recognize their needs as they express them and quickly align them with the services your organization provides. And when things go wrong or don't work, they expect you to know how to fix things—and fix them fast.

Extra Points for Style

A competent physical performed by a rude, disheveled, or distracted physician isn't likely to be a satisfying experience for the patient, regardless of the technical excellence of the practitioner. Once you've mastered the fundamentals of competence, it's your confident style that sets you apart. It starts with first impressions. In their book, *Contact: The First Four Minutes,* Leonard and Natalie Zunin contend that "the first four minutes of any contact is a kind of audition." In some customer service situations, you may have far less time than that—many transactions today are over in twenty to sixty seconds.

But first impressions are only the beginning. In service, everything communicates your style to customers. The way you dress, the way you move, or whether you move at all instead of staying barricaded behind a desk or cash register. The way you talk, the way you do or don't make eye contact, listen, and respond. The way you act when you're not taking care of customers, but still within their view. The way you take care of the person ahead of them in line. All these impressions add up to say, "I know what you need. I can take care of that for you."

Reliable service, delivered quickly and confidently, by knowledgeable, courteous people—what more could your customers want?

> Sayin' it don't make it so. But it ain't braggin' if you can *do* it.
>
> —Don Meredith
> *Monday Night Football*

6

Knock Your Socks Off Service Is:

Empathetic

People don't want to communicate with an "organization" or a computer. They want to talk to a real, live,
responsive, responsible person who will listen and help
them get satisfaction.

—Theo Michelson
Deputy Vice-President, State Farm Insurance

Customers come in a wide variety of shapes and sizes, and
they bring an equally wide variety of wants, needs, expectations, attitudes, and emotions with them to the service transaction. Consequently, customers want to be treated as individuals. No one likes to be treated like a number by a service
worker acting like a machine. Recognizing your customers'
emotional states helps you figure out the best way to effectively and professionally serve them.

Consider how you might treat these two customers if you
were the banquet manager for a fancy hotel:

- Tom Timid walks into the catering office looking ner-
  vous and tense. He is planning a special retirement

party for his boss of ten years and he's obviously never organized a function like this before.
- For Demanding Doris, hosting special events is old hat. The annual sales department gala will be the fourth major event she has organized this year. When she walks into the banquet office, Doris knows exactly what she wants. Her you-all-just-stand-back-and-take-orders attitude is clearly visible.

How do you treat Tom and Doris as individuals? For Tom, it is important to make him comfortable and take the time to make him "feel smart" about the event planning process:

> "Tom, you can depend on me to be there every step of the way. To begin with, why don't you tell me a little bit more about your event, and then I'll show you our step-by-step planning process."

The same technique would probably frustrate, possibly even anger, Doris. She may see your friendly, in-depth explanation as a waste of her valuable time. She expects you to credit her with the savvy she has shown in previous programs:

> "Hello, Doris. It's good to work with you again. I see you brought an outline of everything you need. Let me take a look and see if I have any questions."

Seeing—and treating—each customer as an individual helps you meet the needs of each on their own unique level.

Empathy vs. Sympathy

Whatever the emotional states of your customers, cautious or confident, it's important to them that you understand what they're trying to tell you and how they feel about the services they want you to provide. But when emotions run high, especially when things are going wrong, it is easy to get caught up, even mired, in the emotional world of your customers.

And that can actually hinder your ability to serve customers effectively.

> **TIP:** Nothing positive is ever accomplished when customers and the people trying to serve them cross swords over a problem. When things go wrong, or don't come out quite right, you have to separate the person from the performance—and focus your energy on correcting what went wrong.

When responding to customers' emotions, it is helpful to make a distinction between empathy and sympathy. Both have to do with how you respond to other people's emotions. Many people use the terms interchangeably, but the difference is real and important.

Sympathy involves identifying with, and even taking on, another person's emotions. A sympathetic response is, "I'm really angry about those centerpieces, too."

Empathy means acknowledging and affirming another's emotional state. An empathetic response is, "I can understand how that makes you angry."

> **TIP:** When a service provider wallows in a customer's misfortune, there are two victims instead of one. As a service professional, you need to see the clear difference between what happened and who it happened to—and work on the former to bring things back to normal.

Responding to customers with sympathy puts you on an emotional roller coaster and can leave you worn out and frazzled at the end of the day. The trick is to be emotionally aware and sensitive without becoming too emotionally involved. When you respond with empathy, you stay calm and in control. Only then are you at your absolute best: ready, willing, and able to help your customer.

Showing empathy for customers actually allows you to be professional and caring at the same time. It also makes customers feel like important individuals. Empathy cannot be handed out by a machine; it's something one person does for another. There is no substitute for the human touch you provide when you deliver Knock Your Socks Off Service. That's what makes high quality service such hard work. It's also what makes it so rewarding.

> **TIP:** These days we have less and less human contact. We shop at a supermarket with ten to twenty impersonal checkout lanes. We bank by mail or at an automatic teller, and order our food from drive-up windows. It's no wonder that with all this high tech, customers look for "high touch" from the service people they actually encounter. Use empathy to let your customers know that you—and they—are more than machines.

> **Customers don't care what you know, until they know that you care.**
>
> —Digital Equipment Corp.
> Customer Service Department

7

Knock Your Socks Off Service Is:

Tangibles

From the customer's point of view, if they can see it, walk on it, hold it, hear it, step in it, smell it, carry it, step over it, touch it, use it, even taste it, if they can feel it or sense it, it's customer service.

—SuperAmerica Training Program

Service is difficult to describe in tangible, physical terms. It's fuzzy. Mushy. Slippery. You can't bottle a trip to the movies or an appendectomy any more than you can put a yardstick to advice from a stockbroker or ideas from an interior decorator. Twenty minutes with a physician or auto mechanic isn't necessarily better or worse than ten minutes or thirty minutes. It's the quality of what is accomplished, not the quantity of the time involved. One of the major complications in providing service comes from the fact that so much of it is intangible.

Yet in every service encounter, there are tangibles—before, during, and after the fact—that affect the way customers judge the quality of the service you're providing. If a customer asks for directions in a hotel or strange town and you point, that's intangible. Drawing a map is a way to make the service tangible. The fifth and final key to mastering the fundamentals of Knock Your Socks Off Service is understanding the role tangibles play in making your intangible service memorable and satisfying.

Think about going out to eat:

• *Before* you enter a restaurant, you evaluate it based on some of its tangible attributes: the advertising you've seen or heard, the location as you drive up, and the look of the people who work there. Is the parking lot clean or cluttered with trash? Can you smell the aroma of good food or the remains of half-eaten meals rotting in the dumpster? Do the building and grounds look well-kept? Is the sign lit and legible?

• *As you walk through the front door*, you make more judgments. Does the host or hostess look friendly? Does the establishment appear to be clean? (And if it's not, do you really want to eat the food?) Is there a place to hang your coat? Can you find the restrooms or the telephone without a guide?

• *During* your meal, you evaluate other tangibles, from standard expectations about the menu and the tableware to unique items such as the special hat you see a waitress give a small child or the balloons passed out to a group celebrating a birthday. You judge the way your food is presented—how it looks on the plate and how closely it resembles the wonderful picture you saw on the menu—as well as how it tastes.

• *Afterward*, there are still more forms of tangible evidence for you to weigh. When the bill arrives, is it clean, accurate, and clearly understandable, or do you get the impression that it absorbed more of your meal than you did? If you use the restroom, is it clean? And if you dined at Bridgeman's Ice Cream Parlor and finished off your meal with the famous La La Palooza Sundae, do you walk out the door with your I DID IT! button?

Demonstrating Value

Tangibles help convey the value of the service transaction's intangible aspects. They're an important way for you to educate your customers and help them evaluate the quality of service you've provided. Manage the tangible aspects of the encounter and you give your customers something solid to tie their impressions to.

> **TIP:** If you're helping a customer estimate the cost of a purchase, be it a new stereo system or a roomful of carpet, write your calculations neatly on a page with your name and phone number. Your customer will appreciate having it as a reference and will easily remember who provided such terrific service.

The best rule of thumb regarding the tangibles you manage is, Never give something to customers you'd be reluctant, embarrassed, or angered to receive yourself. Here are three ways you can demonstrate the value of the service transaction:

1. Take pride in your own appearance and the look and feel of the materials you give to your customer. Hand them over personally instead of tossing them on a countertop or leaving it to the customer to figure out what to gather up and how to organize and carry them.

2. When customers give you their name, phone number, or other information, write it down. This demonstrates that you think the information is important. And make a point of getting it right—read it back to make sure there's no mistake.
3. Make sure the parts of your workplace customers see—and especially those they touch—are clean, safe, and as comfortable as you can make them.

When your customers describe your service to their friends and colleagues—people who could become your next customers—they will focus on their observations of tangible things. To keep customers coming back again and again, you want those tangibles to reflect well on you and the service you provide.

First impressions are the most lasting.

—Proverb

8

Customers Are Everywhere—Inside and Out

X If you're not serving the customer, your job is to be serving someone who is.

—Jan Carlzon
CEO, Scandinavian Airlines System

Service doesn't just happen on the frontline, where service providers come face-to-face with customers as consumers. In fact, you may never see the customers who ultimately buy and use the products and services your company provides. Does that make you any less of a service professional? Not on your life. Everyone has a customer, just as everyone is a customer.

There are two basic types of customers:

1. *External customers.* The people who buy your products and services. They are external to, or outside of, your company; they are the source of the revenue that funds continuing operations. Without them, you won't be in business for very long.
2. *Internal customers.* The people who work for your organization. Regardless of whether they are at another

location in your building, in another state or country,
or sitting at the next desk in your department, if they
depend on you and the work you do in order to
complete their own work, often so they can serve their
own customers—*they* are your customers.

There's a remarkably close and consistent link between
how internal customers are treated and how external customers perceive the quality of your organization's services. Benja-
min Schneider, professor of psychology and business management at the University of Maryland, is well known for his
research on how "the people make the place." He notes that a
commitment to serve internal customers invariably shows
itself to external customers, and that it's almost impossible to
provide good external service if your organization is not
providing good internal service. Without a commitment to
high-quality, Knock Your Socks Off Service inside an organization, service to end-user consumers will surely suffer.

Identifying Your Customers

When Jan Carlzon led the remarkable turnaround that brought
Scandinavian Airlines System (SAS) from an $8 million loss
in 1981 to a gross profit of $71 million in 1982, he didn't
resort to new advertising or clever accounting gimmicks. He
did it by inspiring an uncompromising focus on the customer
at every level of the airline. Part of that focus involved changing the way people within SAS saw and interacted with other
SAS employees.

Carlzon's service strategy was to make SAS the best possible air travel choice for business travelers. To do that, he
believed that every employee of the airline had to focus on
customer service. But Carlzon knew that not everyone in the
company had direct interaction with external customers: the
passengers boarding the planes. In fact, a very significant
portion of SAS employees served only internal customers:

- Maintenance workers made it possible for ground crews
  and pilots to keep the planes flying on time.

- Catering staff kept the planes well-stocked with food and beverages so flight attendants could keep passengers fed and comfortable.
- And managers had to do whatever it took to serve their frontline people so that they, in turn, could serve passengers.

To make sure everyone knew where they stood in the new SAS, Carlzon proclaimed a simple, universal job description: "If you aren't serving the customer, your job is to be serving someone who is." That told everyone, from the frontlines to management, that the airline could only survive if they all worked together to make the organization function on their passengers' behalf. It also told everyone where to focus their efforts: on service.

Internal Customers

External customers are pretty easy to identify. Sometimes, however, it's difficult to identify your customers when they are inside your organization. Maybe you don't see them face-to-face. Maybe you're not sure what happens to your work when it leaves your desk or department. Maybe the same people you serve also serve you. The customer/service provider relationship within an organization is not static. It can change from day to day, from moment to moment.

> **TIP:** How can you figure out who's who? At Dun & Bradstreet, the financial information company, people identify their customers, whether internal or external, by asking two simple questions:
>
> 1. Where does my work go?
> 2. Who is my work important to?

At Dun & Bradstreet, everybody has a customer, no matter where on the organizational ladder they may be. In your organization, your customer is whoever benefits from the work you do—or, conversely, whoever suffers when your work is done poorly or not at all.

If, for example, you take customer orders at your company's telephone center, obviously you are serving external customers directly. But you have internal customers, too. Who receives the orders you take from those external customers? What happens when necessary information is missing from those orders, or is entered incorrectly? The impact of what you do or don't do affects both your external customers, who may not receive what they ordered, and your internal customers in the warehouse, billing, and shipping, who will have to deal with the complaint that comes when the order isn't received.

> **TIP:** Once you've identified your customers, talk to them about what they do and don't like about the service you provide for them. Use their feedback to improve the quality of the work you do.

Customers truly are everywhere, outside your organization as well as within. It is your job to identify your customers, to know what they need from you and how you can provide it for them. Doing so in ways that maximize both internal and external customer satisfaction is what creates that sense of teamwork and camaraderie that good organizations thrive on.

Serving customers requires 360-degree vision.

—Sign above a warehouse manager's desk

9

The Ten Deadly Sins of Customer Service

Would *you* do business with you?

> —Linda Silverman Goldzimer
> *"I'm First": Your Customer's Message to You*

Everyone has pet peeves, things that irritate and annoy. When you were young, knowing what set off your little brother or sister could afford you hours of pleasure. As adults, we recognize that annoying habits and behaviors are not only bad manners, they also can get you into serious trouble—especially on the job.

Knock Your Socks Off Service is a positive philosophy. But part of serving well is knowing what not to do. It's impossible to anticipate everything that might get under the skin of a particular customer. But there are things that irritate almost all of us when we're on the customer side of the counter. Avoid these irritants for your own sake as well as your customer's.

Here are ten "sins" you can control, behaviors and actions that some service providers (never you or us!) exhibit that customers say annoy them most. While our list is based largely on our research with customers and service professionals, as well as on our own experience as customers, we're also indebted to Karl Albrecht's book, *At America's Service.*

Ten Sins You Can Control

1. *"I don't know."* A survey of retail customers in Washington, D.C., found the number one reason for switching to catalog shopping was that salespeople in stores were so ignorant about the merchandise. Customers expect you to know something about the products and services you sell. If you really can't answer a customer's question, add three essential words to the sentence above: "I'll find out."

2. *"I don't care."* Customers want you to care about serving them. They want to sense that you take pride in what you're doing. This reinforces that they've made a good choice by doing business with you. When your attitude, conversation, or appearance makes it clear you'd rather be somewhere else, they'll find themselves wishing the same thing.

3. *"I can't be bothered."* Actions really do speak louder than words. Believe it. If your conversation with a co-worker or an obviously personal phone call takes precedence over a customer, or you studiously ignore someone's attempt to catch your attention, your customers will be annoyed—and rightfully so.

4. *"I don't like you."* Customers are sensitive to attitudes that subtly or overtly say, "You're a nuisance; please go away." And no one enjoys the occasional encounter with a customer service person who is openly (or even snidely) hostile. The more aggressively obnoxious your behavior, the more memorable it will be for your customer, for all the wrong reasons.

5. *"I know it all."* When you jump in with a solution or comment before a customer has finished explaining his or her problem or question, that's being pushy. So, too, is trying to force a customer to make a buying decision. Knowledge is a tool to help you serve customers better, not a bludgeon with which to beat them into submission.

6. *"You don't know anything."* There are no dumb questions, only dumb answers. When you rudely or insensitively

cut off, put down, or demean customers for having a confused or wrong idea of what exactly they need or what you can do for them, you slam the door in their face. Next time, they'll look for another door to walk their business through.

7. *"We don't want your kind here."* Prejudice, like customers, comes in all shapes, sizes, ages, colors, educational levels, and any other characteristic you care to name. But regardless of class or category, every customer is an individual who wants (and deserves) to be treated with courtesy and respect. Do you treat customers who show up in suits better than those who dress in jeans and T-shirts? Do you assume that elderly customers won't be able to understand complex issues, or that younger customers aren't seriously interested in buying anything? Your attitudes show in ways you may never even suspect.

8. *"Don't come back."* The purpose of serving customers well is to convince them to come back again and again. The easiest way to discourage that is to make it clear in words or actions that they're an inconvenience in your day you'd just as soon be rid of once and for all. Thanking customers for their patronage and loyalty builds a relationship that can grow and mature.

9. *"I'm right and you're wrong."* One of the easiest (and most human) traps to fall into is arguing with a customer over something that really is more a point of personal pride or pique than professional service. Customers are not always right, of course, but it doesn't cost you anything to give them the benefit of the doubt.

10. *"Hurry up and wait."* More than any other variable, time may be the number one obsession for people today. Everyone starts with only twenty-four hours a day; no one wants to waste any of it, whether waiting for something to take place or being forced into a hasty decision that they'll sooner or later come to regret. Respect your customer's time and you'll find they respect you in return.

Baber's Rules of Customer Service

Make the customers feel heard.
Make the customers understood.
Make the customers liked.
Make the customers respected.
Make the customers feel helped.
Make the customers appreciated
and respected.

—Michael Baber
*Integrated Business Leadership Through
Cross Marketing*

10

The Customer Is Always . . . The Customer

Our Policy
Rule 1: The customer is always right!
Rule 2: If the customer is ever wrong, reread Rule 1.

—Stew Leonard's Dairy Store
Norwalk, Connecticut

These words, chiseled into a 6,000-pound rock resting just outside the front door of Stew Leonard's, the world's largest (and most profitable) dairy store, are probably familiar.

They are also wrong.

So why does a successful and intelligent businessman like Stew Leonard proclaim "Rule 1" and "Rule 2" at the entrance to his store? Because he—and each of his employees—knows, lives, and breathes the real truth behind the slogan writ on the rock: Customers are not always right, but they are *always* our customers.

Right and Wrong

The customer is not always right. You know it. We know it. In fact, studies conducted by Washington, D.C.-based TARP Insti-

39

tute, a premier service research firm, even prove it scientifi-
cally. TARP finds that customers cause about a third of the
service and product problems they complain about. Blindly
believing, or acting as if you believe the customer is always
right, can be detrimental to you and to your customer.

Customers-are-always-right thinking can put a stop to
problem solving and customer education. You can't correct a
problem or a customer's misconception if you can't admit that
it exists. Many times when customers cause problems—or
believe untrue things—it's because we haven't taught them
any different. We are so familiar with the products we sell and
the services we supply that we forget how much there is to
know, how much we have to help our customers learn.

Perhaps more dangerous is that customers-are-always-
right thinking puts service providers in a one-down position.
It says, "You're not paid to think or ask questions. Just smile
and do whatever the customer tells you to do." No wonder
that in such settings, service begins to feel like servitude:
"Hello, my name is Pat and I'll be your personal servant this
evening."

Finally, blindly holding to the idea that customers are
always right means that when something goes wrong—as it
will, sooner or later—you must be wrong. You know that's not
true. If you're behind the counter in a McDonald's and a
customer walks up and orders McLobster and a bottle of
McChampagne, it's very clear who's right and who's wrong.
It's also irrelevant. Your job is to manage the experience so the
customer eventually is right and remains your customer.

Why We're There

The customer is our only reason for being there. Knowing that
the customer is always the customer (not the problem, the
enemy, or the bane of your existence) helps focus your effort
where it belongs—on keeping the customer. The goal of every
service transaction is, and must be, to satisfy and delight
customers in ways that will keep them coming back for more.

As a service professional, you hold the power to make

that happen. To do it, you need to be and act smart. You need to know more than your customer does about the products and services you sell and supply. You need to be sensitive to the fact that customers, like service professionals, are only human, with human faults and feelings. When customers are wrong, your role is to use your skills to help make them right, in a manner that neither embarrasses nor blames.

Three Ways to Make Customers Right

1. *Assume innocence.* "Guilty until proved innocent" doesn't play well with customers. Just because what they are saying sounds wrong to you, don't assume that it is. It may be that they are simply explaining what they need or want poorly, or that the directions they should have received were missing or misleading.

> "I see what happened. The computer disk is copy-protected, which is why it froze up when you tried to copy it onto your hard drive. Unfortunately, the directions assume that you know that will happen. Here's how we can fix things for you. . . ."

2. *Look for teaching opportunities.* What information could your customers have used before the misunderstanding occurred? Make sure they get it now.

> "I'm glad you brought this to my attention. The information you needed was here in your packet, but I can see how it would be easy to miss, buried under so many other papers. Let's review your packet to see if I can head off any other surprises."

3. *Believe your customer.* Sometimes, the customer you initially think is 100 percent wrong will turn out to be right after all. If you've ridden roughshod over their request or complaint, you're going to find yourself wolfing down a heaping helping of Humble Pie. The point of Knock Your Socks Off

Service is to keep customer relationships intact. When in doubt, give your customer the benefit of the doubt.

> "Let's check the advertising flyer to verify that the price you saw is for this model. Sure enough, there it is. Thanks for pointing that out to me. I'll make sure we get the shelf tags corrected so everyone knows which model is on sale."

Unfair Advantage

What about customers who try to use your service standards against you and get something for nothing, or a better deal than they are entitled to? First, it's important to recognize that truly dishonest customers are pretty rare. But they do exist. And they are your customers.

We recommend the "Three Strikes and You're Out" policy used by Stuart Skorman, president of Empire Video of Keene, New Hampshire. The first time a customer and clerk disagree on whether a video was returned, "it must have been our mistake," Skorman says. Same thing the second time. But three strikes, and the customer's credibility is gone.

> Don't find a fault. Find a remedy.
>
> —Henry Ford

The How To's of Knock Your Socks Off Service

Outstanding customer service is made up of important, individual actions. Each is relatively easy and simple to master. All combine to make the service you provide truly memorable.

How well you listen, understand, and respond to each customer . . . how you handle face-to-face contact . . . how you use the telephone . . . the words you put on paper . . . the way you anticipate a customer's needs . . . and whether you thank them for doing business with you . . . all contribute to your customer's evaluation of your efforts.

Properly combined and skillfully executed, these elements add up to outstanding service, the kind that says, "I'm gonna knock your socks off!"

11

Honesty Is the
Only Policy

*A man always has two reasons for doing anything — a
good reason, and the real reason.*

—J. P. Morgan
Financier

When it comes to customer service, honesty isn't the best
policy, it is the only policy. Lying to, or misleading, customers
invariably leads to far worse problems than looking them
straight in the eye and telling them something unpleasant they
need to hear right now.

There are two very good reasons for facing your customer
with the bad news.

First, tall tales inevitably catch up with you, and often in
the most unexpected ways. Thomas Connellan, a good friend
and insightful consultant, tells the story of a shipping clerk
(let's call him Ralph) in a company in Michigan who had
discovered a cute and, to his way of thinking, foolproof way of
keeping customers off his back. Every morning he would bring
three newspapers to work: the *New York Daily News*, the
Chicago Tribune, and the *Los Angeles Times*. He would scan
each carefully and circle any news item having to do with a
transportation disaster—train wrecks and derailments, heavy

snowfall in the Rocky Mountains, trucking strikes in the Southeast—you get the picture.

Then, for the rest of the day, any time a customer called up complaining that a promised shipment had not yet arrived, Ralph would put the caller on hold, thumb through the newspapers until he found a likely item, go back to the caller and ask: "Did you hear about the train that derailed outside Forth Worth last night? No? Well, it happened, and I know for a fact that your shipment was on that train. I'd like to help you out, but there's not a thing I can do about a natural disaster."

Ralph's little trick worked well for all of a year—until a purchasing agent customer, suspicious of the fact that three of his last five promised shipments were subject to "natural disasters," began checking around. To make a long story short, he figured out what Ralph was up to, put Ralph's company on his "Unreliable Vendor" list, and wrote a stinging letter to Ralph's company president. Do you need to ask what kind of natural disaster happened to Ralph?

The second reason for playing straight with your customers is that—surprise!—customers respect honesty. No, it isn't fun to tell a customer that there is a problem, or that the delivery date the customer has in mind is unrealistic. But when you have to, and make it clear you will follow through to do all in your power to make things right again, your customers come away appreciating you as a straight shooter that they can depend on to tell the truth—regardless.

Miss Manners, aka Judith Martin, dubbed The High Priestess of Protocol by *Frequent Flyer* magazine, provides a case in point. She described two recent airline flights, both delayed due to bad weather. As she described them to the readers of *Frequent Flyer*:

> On the first, the crew did little to inform the passengers of the flight's status, glumly responding to requests for pillows, blankets, drinks, etc. The second crew apologized for the delay, offered advice on passengers' scheduling problems, kept everyone informed, and generally tried to make things as pleasant as possible.

Which planeload of passengers believed that the flight crew was really doing everything possible to get them to their destination? And which airline will Miss Manners choose the next time she flies?

Do It for You, Too

There is actually a third reason for always being honest with customers: the way you feel about yourself. A friend of ours used to work for one of those television shopping network companies. She was the chief upset customer handler. When customers called in to report that the merchandise they bought was defective, her job was to smother those callers with "I'm sorry" and "We apologize" verbiage.

The trouble was, most of the merchandise the company was selling was factory seconds—items known by everyone in the company to be defective. Our friend was, in essence, a shill charged with the responsibility of mollifying the few customers who were brave enough to complain about their purchases. The company, she was told straight out, was counting on the fact that only about 4 percent of upset customers complain when they receive shoddy service or merchandise.

Did she give the complainers their money back? Absolutely. The company was willing to buy off the few who braved its complaint and return systems. Did she make the complainers feel better? Definitely. At least someone was there to listen to them.

But she quit her job after six months. Why? "Because," she says, "I couldn't take being part of a sleazy operation that was knowingly exploiting its customers."

> **TIP:** How you feel about yourself in your job is as important to your personal self-esteem as the way you feel about yourself as a parent, a spouse, or a friend. No job is important enough to lie for, no paycheck big enough to compensate for feeling bad about your treatment of another human being. Perhaps the best reason to be honest with your customers is that it allows you to be honest with yourself.

> **Whoever is careless with the truth in small matters cannot be trusted with important matters.**
>
> —Albert Einstein

12

Do the Right Thing . . . Regardless

Use your good judgment in all situations.
There will be no additional rules.

—Nordstrom, Inc., Employee Handbook

Doing the right thing and doing things right are separate but related issues in providing Knock Your Socks Off Service.

Doing things right deals with knowing—developing and using technical skills and people skills, knowing about your customers' needs and expectations, learning about your company's products and services, and being able to answer questions about how things work and why.

Doing the right thing is action-oriented. It involves making judgments about how to use your company's products and services on your customers' behalf—sometimes in ways they may not have asked for, or even thought of.

The Nordstrom Department Stores' Employee Handbook is, by now, almost legendary. Its elegantly simple, solitary rule is: Use your good judgment in all situations. The lack of additional rules doesn't mean there's no direction. Nordstrom employees—those fabled Knock Your Socks Off Service professionals—are encouraged to use their managers for support when they're not sure what to do. In Nordstrom's words:

"Please feel free to ask your department manager,
store manager or division general manager any question at any time."

In orientation and training programs, Nordstrom people
learn what doing the right thing means for the customers they
will serve. Sometimes it means accepting a return with no
questions asked or walking a customer to another department—even to a competitor's store—to find just the right
clothing accessory. The result? From coast to coast, people tell
stories about service, Nordstrom style. Even those who've
never seen the inside of a Nordstrom store (the company
operates mostly on the West Coast) have heard the stories.
And just about the time they start to shake their heads and say
things like, "Sure, but how long can they stay in business
doing things like that?" someone adds the real clincher:

▲ Nordstrom regularly posts the highest sales per
   square foot in the retail industry. Not only does nobody do it better, nobody makes more money doing
   it right, either!

Is the Right Thing Ever Wrong?

Many frontline service workers and plenty of managers feel
an instinctive fear of simple policies such as, "do the right
thing." The fear is natural; for generations, we've been warned
about the dire consequences of "giving the store away." But
that fear is easily overcome when common sense and the
competence that comes with experience are brought to bear
on the subject.

Are you going to give the store away? Of course not, no
more than Nordstrom's people do. When managers and service
professionals feel uncertain about the idea of "do the right
thing," we tell them the point of Knock Your Socks Off Service
is to delight their customers. That makes customers come back
again—and that makes money for the company.

It's pointless for your company to hire good people, train

them well, back them with customer-friendly systems and supportive management, only to refuse them the opportunity (or see them decline the opportunity) to make good judgments on their customers' behalf. The system's not out of control; it is being controlled by *your* innate good sense. That's why your company has already entrusted you with its most price-less asset—customers, the very future of the business.

Your own good judgment applies in every industry. At the North Carolina-based Duke Power Company, which operates nuclear power plants, employees are both highly skilled and extensively trained. Then they are turned loose to work on behalf of the company and its customers. As part of new employee orientation, each person receives a letter from Chairman and CEO Bill Lee explaining what to do if they are ever in a position where doing what the customer wants and needs is in conflict with a company rule or policy: "Ask why [the rule exists]. If the answer is not compelling, do what you think is right. It probably will be."

Bill Lee's people know their job and he knows they know it. His letter is written acknowledgment that doing the job well means doing the right thing. Through the letter, Bill Lee gives employees his official permission to work for their customers. It's that approach to Knock Your Socks Off Service that consistently makes Duke Power one of the best-run, safest, and most respected in its industry.

> **TIP:** Make a point of getting together with your co-workers. Share stories of times you or they did the right thing for customers. What can you learn from those experiences?

Even though your company faces different challenges than Nordstrom, and your managers have different styles than Bill Lee, doing the right thing is no less a part of your role as a service professional. If you know your job but aren't exactly sure what you can and cannot do, take a page from the Nordstrom handbook and Lee's orientation letter: Ask for guidance.

> If they [employees] make a wrong decision, that's something that can be corrected later. At least they acted in good faith. This is part of our commitment [to our customers].
>
> —Isadore Sharp
> Chairman, Four Seasons Hotels

13

Listening Is a Skill— Use It

Listening is about trust and respect and involvement and information sharing more than it is about ears.

— Beverly Briggs
Editor, *Customer Connection Newsletter*

Most of us listen to only about 25 percent of what we hear. What happens to the other 75 percent? We tune it out. In one ear and out the other, it's as if we never heard it. Listening is so important, it's amazing how seldom we practice it well. But since good service involves listening, understanding, and responding to customers, good listening is an important skill for practitioners of Knock Your Socks Off Service. Why?

- It helps you figure out what your customer wants and needs.
- It can prevent misunderstandings and errors.
- It gives you clues about ways to improve the service you provide.
- It helps build long-term customer relationships.

It's important to listen actively, almost aggressively. To serve your customers well, you need to know as exactly as possible what they want, how they want it, when they want it, what they expect to pay for it, how long they expect to wait, and what else they expect with it. There's no need to guess—and risk being wrong. Your customer is ready, willing, and able to tell you everything (or almost everything) you need to know.

Good Listeners Are Made, Not Born

People who seem to be natural listeners weren't born that way. They just started practicing a lot earlier. It's never too late to start improving because good listening is a skill that gets better as you exercise it. What's more, the listener has a powerful advantage in any conversation: While most people speak at only 125 to 150 words per minute, we can listen at up to 450 words per minute! That means we have time while listening to identify the main points the speaker is trying to make and begin to organize those points into an effective response.

> **TIP:** Reinforce listening to your customer by writing down information and ideas on how to respond—but don't dilute your focus by trying to formulate a rebuttal or argument. When you have a chance to speak, you will be able to "reflect" back your customer's key points. Reflection, even of the easy and obvious things, confirms that you have listened and understood your customer and are now ready to respond to the request, question, or problem.

Make sure you hear what the speaker is trying to communicate:

1. If the information is complex, confirm your understanding by repeating it: "Okay. Let me catch up with you. You've made some important points and I want to make sure I understand. You said that you. . . ."
2. Ask questions if you are unclear about anything: "Do you want the multi-faceted jumbo widget with the

reverse locking knob or the super-faceted mini model with the glow-in-the-dark handle?"

3. Repeat critical (to the customer) information, for example, the spelling of the company's name or the numbers in an address or phone number.

A wide variety of distractions can get in the way of good listening.

Barriers to Effective Listening

• *Noise.* Too much noise in your business environment causes interference. Can you easily hear customers when they speak in a normal tone of voice? Or are they drowned out by too-loud music, the general hubbub of your workplace, or the voices of your co-workers and other customers?

• *Interruptions.* Communication happens when two people work at it together. Have you ever tried to explain something to someone who was constantly saying, "Just a sec, gotta take this call" or looking over your shoulder to yell advice or information to a colleague? Such controllable interruptions tell customers, "You aren't important" or, "I really don't want to listen to you."

• *Daydreaming.* Interruptions come from inside as well as outside. When you find your thoughts drifting away to the movie you plan to see tonight, or the fight you had with your spouse this morning, that internal interruption can be every bit as destructive to good listening. Keep the focus on your customer.

• *Technology.* Technology can hinder effective listening as much as it can help to put us in touch. For all the service made possible by telephones, voice-activated terminals, and remote microphones in drive-up windows, it's much harder to listen to someone you can't see face-to-face, or whose voice is distorted by a machine.

• *Stereotypes.* When we label people, when we make assumptions about what they look like, how they will behave, and what they have to say, we make it difficult to understand what they're really saying. From that false start, we fit what we later see, experience, and hear into a flawed prejudgment. And quite often we're very wrong.

• *Trigger words and phrases.* All of us have hot-buttons that customers may inadvertently push. And once the button is pushed, listening can stop. Remember that your main concern is to listen to what your customer is trying to say, not the individual words he or she uses. What rubs you the wrong way just may be completely innocent from the customer's perspective. (And even if the customer is giving you a dig over past performance, letting it pass shows your good grace and style.)

• *Attitude.* Your attitudes color what you hear and how you respond. Defensive people evaluate everything, looking for the hidden messages. People on the offensive are too often looking for a fight, formulating oh-yes-well-let-me-tell-you arguments even before the other person is finished speaking. Your attitudes should help you listen, not deafen you to a customer's words.

It's also important to listen for the things that you don't hear, the things your customers aren't saying to you. If customers used to compliment you on speedy delivery, but haven't recently, perhaps your performance is slipping. If they sigh and say, "Oh, fine, I guess," when you ask them how your services measure up, you should be hearing another message loud and clear.

> You can tell more about a person by what he says about others than you can by what others say about him.
>
> —Dale Carnegie
> Author and educator

14

Winning Words and Soothing Phrases

Politeness goes far, yet costs nothing.

—Samuel Smiles
Nineteenth-century popular writer

"Oh yeah?! Sticks and stones may break my bones, but words will never hurt me." Sound familiar? As children, we recited those words many times. They were our self-defense in the very situations where we learned that words did hurt—emotionally, if not physically. And many of us carry memories that remind us that the pain words inflict can be more devastating than any bruise or broken arm.

Words are just as powerful to adults. We are capable of bruising or soothing our customers with words; it all depends on how we use them. The service professional who can use words well gains a distinct advantage in the service transaction.

Forbidden Phrases

Some words, alone or in combination, create immediate negative images. Nancy Friedman, a customer service and telephone skills consultant known to many by her business persona, The Telephone "Doctor,"™ advocates the ban on what she calls Five Forbidden Phrases—five responses that, intentionally or unintentionally, can drive your customers right up the wall in anger or frustration. Here they are, with her suggested alternatives:

Forbidden Phrase	Use Instead
1. I don't know.	"Gee, that's a good question. Let me check and find out."
2. We can't do that.	"Boy, that's a tough one. Let's see what we can do." Then find an alternative solution.
3. *You'll* have to. . . .	Soften the request with phrases like, "You'll need to," or "Here's how we can help you with that," or "The next time that happens, here's what you can do."
4. Hang on a second: I'll be right back.	"It may take me two or three minutes [*or however long it will really take*] to get that. Are you able to hold/wait while I check?"
5. *No* when used at the beginning of any sentence.	If you think before you speak, you can turn every answer into a positive response. "We aren't able to refund your money, but we can replace the product at no charge."

While those five phrases are sure to raise customer ire, they aren't the only ones. Which ones not on the list above would rile you as a customer?

TIP: Take a piece of paper and start your own helpful checklist. Ask two or three of your co-workers about the phrases or statements that make them angry or upset as a customer. Add those phrases, too. In a very short amount of time, you'll realize how many simple, everyday sayings can take on extra meaning when viewed in the light of our experiences as customers.

The Message Behind the Words

Every Knock Your Socks Off Service professional has times when something said in all sincerity or innocence to a customer, something that sounds reasonable and rational to you, causes the customer to explode with anger. It's not the intent of your words to create customer anger, but it is the effect. As you learn to notice some of the common words and phrases that provoke these undesirable responses, you'll find yourself becoming more successful at avoiding or defusing such situations.

One of the most common negative messages we can send to customers is, "I think you're stupid." We send that message when we use phrases like, "Do you understand?" or when we begin talking to a customer as if we were addressing a four-year-old (even though the customer's behavior may be straight out of preschool). If four-year-olds don't appreciate being talked down to, why should adult customers find it enjoyable or satisfying?

A helpful technique to ensure understanding without demeaning the customer was described by Beverly Briggs in the *Customer Connection Newsletter*. She described the technique used by a cable TV technician to make sure the customer on the phone was starting from the right point:

> Before I can help [a subscriber] with a problem, it's important for me to confirm that the set is tuned in to the right channel. . . . When I ask "Is the TV tuned to channel 3?" the customer answers "Yes" automatically . . . and I'm uncomfortable saying "Please go

and check." So now I say, "Will you please go to the
TV set and turn it to channel 5. Wait for ten seconds
then turn it back to channel 3. Then come back and
tell me what happened." This gets the action I need
without having to challenge the customer's word.

He also doesn't communicate that he thinks the customer
really doesn't know how to operate a TV.

Helpful Responses

What words and phrases are guaranteed to bring a smile to
your customer's face? We've made a list, but it's just a start.
From your own experience and the insight of your co-workers,
you can add many more of your own. Put them with your
checklist of customer-annoying phrases as a reminder to use
these whenever you can:

> "Good morning"—or afternoon or evening, said as if you
> mean it.
> 'Thank you."
> "Consider it done," "I'll do that immediately," or "I'll
> take care of that for you."
> "Certainly, sir"—or ma'am, or the individual's name.
> "I understand how you feel"—when you do understand.
> "I take full responsibility."
> "No problem"—the only exception to Forbidden Phrase
> #5 (starting a sentence with no).

Man does not live by words alone, despite the fact that
sometimes he has to eat them.

—Adlai Stevenson
Lawyer and politician

15

Facts for
Face-to-Face

Customer service means projecting a positive image.

—Anonymous

The words we speak, hear, or read are only a small part of the way we communicate with one another. Experts suggest that in face-to-face situations, at least 70 percent of what is communicated is done without speaking a word. This is called nonverbal communication.

What is nonverbal communication? It's everything we don't say—our body language, what we do, how we act and react, and what we show to others when we are with them. There are nine basic dimensions of nonverbal communication. Knock Your Socks Off Service professionals are keenly aware of each.

1. *Proximity*. Carry on a conversation with a co-worker while standing about an arm's length apart. After a few minutes, move forward until your noses are about six inches apart. Feel uncomfortable? Most North Americans will. The same will be true if you're standing six feet apart. "Comfort zones" vary from culture to culture. Most North Americans prefer to maintain a distance of between a foot and a half and two feet.

2. *Eye contact*. Making eye contact acknowledges that

you see, and are dealing with, your customers as individuals, that you are paying attention. There's a balance to be struck here: People who don't make eye contact in our culture are considered shifty or even dishonest, but staring can make your customers uncomfortable, too.

3. *Silence.* You can and do communicate even when you're saying nothing. Remaining silent while your customers are talking is a basic courtesy, nodding tells them you're listening and understanding what you hear. Prolonged silence, however, can leave customers concerned that either you did not hear them or that you disagree with what they said. An occasional "uh huh" or "I see" tells them you're still listening without interrupting.

4. *Gestures.* Closed gestures such as tightly crossed arms, hands tucked deep in pockets or clenched fists, create nonverbal barriers. Open gestures invite people into our space and say we're comfortable having them near us. Many of our gestures are unconscious (some people cross their arms when they're cold, for example), so make a point of thinking about what you're doing nonverbally when you deal with customers.

5. *Posture.* "Stand up straight," your mother always said, and she was right. Good physical posture conveys confidence and competence. Leaning in slightly when customers are

talking says you think what they're saying is important and interesting.

6. *Facial expression.* We all know the cues: A raised eyebrow communicates surprise; a wink, sly agreement or alliance; tightly set lips, opposition; a wide open smile, friendliness. Your face communicates, even when your voice doesn't.

7. *Physical contact.* What is and is not appropriate today varies greatly with the situation and the people involved. A handshake is customary, but placing a hand on another person's arm or an arm over someone's shoulder can be a very personal act. The rule of thumb is "less is best" in most professional situations.

8. *Smell.* This is perhaps the least understood of our senses, but an important one in service work that involves getting close to customers. Be just as careful with strong perfumes and colognes—some customers may be sensitive or allergic—as you are of the natural odors they are used to cover up. Be aware, too, that at a time when fewer than one in three adults smokes, the lingering smell of tobacco can be offensive.

9. *Overall appearance.* Just as in a theatrical performance, you have to look your part. Whether your costume is a three-piece suit or blue coveralls depends on the job you do, what you want to communicate to customers, and especially what your customers expect to see. Whatever the case, one thing will always be true of your physical appearance: Cleanliness and neatness communicate competence. (Messy people may be just as, if not more, competent than neat people, it's true, but they will have to work a lot harder to prove it to the customer!)

TIP: Sometimes the nonverbal messages we send are more powerful, more persuasive, and more revealing than the words we speak. When our nonverbal signals send a different message than our words, our customers can become confused, disoriented, or skeptical of our motives, actions, and interest in serving their needs. A significant part of your success as a service professional will come from how you manage your face-to-face, nonverbal communications.

Nonverbal Cues

The flip side of nonverbal communication is knowing how to read the nonverbal cues of your customers. Almost everyone can look at other people and read their obvious body language. We know when others are happy or sad, calm or upset.

What makes one person appear so at ease in social situations or in dealing with customers, while others seem uncomfortable, unaware or inept? Research suggests that the difference may lie in what we do with what we know. Socially adept individuals more readily accept and act on the body language signals they see. Others plow blindly ahead, unmindful of the confused looks that say, "Please stop and explain that again."

Customers may not always speak up when they feel uncomfortable or confused or frustrated. But if you "listen" for the messages, you pick up the nonverbal cues as well as the audible ones. Use them effectively and they'll help you meet and exceed your customer's needs and expectations.

Perception is the key to nonverbal success.

—Sales training axiom

16

Tips for Telephone Talk

If I pick up a ringing phone, I accept the responsibility to ensure the caller is satisfied, no matter what the issue.

—Michael Ramundo
President, MCR Marketing, Inc.

The telephone requires you to be more aware of your voice than at any other time. Customers cannot hear your facial expressions or your overall physical appearance, but they do form a mental picture of you based on the tone and quality of your voice. Your mood—smiling and happy or tight-lipped and angry—often comes through. That's why, before you ever pick up a telephone, you should take a moment to be sure that you are mentally prepared to deal with the customer on the other end. A pleasant phone voice takes practice. This Telephone Style Checklist (see box) can help you assess your phone style. After all, speaking in well-modulated, pleasant tones is a learned talent.

TIP: Tape yourself talking on the phone, then ask an honest friend or your boss to evaluate your vocal quality. Better yet, have someone tape you from the listener's end so you can listen to how you sound to your customers.

WARNING: If you have never heard yourself on audio-tape before, you will be surprised at the way you sound. Don't let it bother you: We all sound strange to ourselves on tape.

TELEPHONE STYLE CHECKLIST

Vocal Quality

Yes	No	
☐	☐	Voice is easy to hear without being too loud.
☐	☐	Words are clearly articulated.
☐	☐	Pacing is good—neither too slow nor too fast.
☐	☐	Vocal tone is pleasant—neither grating nor nasal.
☐	☐	Energy level shows interest and enthusiasm.

Phone Techniques

Yes	No	
☐	☐	Phone is answered quickly—on the second or third ring.
☐	☐	Caller is greeted courteously.
☐	☐	Representative identifies self to caller.
☐	☐	Transfers are handled professionally.
☐	☐	Messages taken are complete and accurate.

Telephone Etiquette: A Quick Review

Professional telephone talk has its rules. Knowing and following them will ensure that your customers feel you are really taking care of them.

Answering the Phone

The ringing of a telephone is one of the most insistent sounds in the world. (Just try to let your home phone ring without answering it. Most people can't.) When a customer calls and no one answers, or the line is busy, or it rings fifteen times before someone picks it up, it's like telling the customer (as one phone company's television ad says), "I'm sorry, but you will have to take your money and leave the store. We are very busy here and we just don't have time to help you. Please go shop somewhere else. And thank you for trying to do business with us." Set a standard for yourself (two or three rings, for example) and try to meet it every time.

> **TIP:** When you answer the phone, greet the customer with "good morning" or "good afternoon." Even "hello" will work nicely. Then identify yourself and your company. The caller doesn't automatically know who will pick up the phone.

Putting a Caller on Hold

Sometimes callers have to be put on hold: You may need to answer a second line, you may need to leave your desk to get a piece of information, or you may just need a moment to regroup while handling a particularly volatile caller.

Whatever the circumstances, never put a caller on hold without first asking permission—"May I put you on hold?" or, "Will you hold, please?" And the question means nothing if you don't wait for the answer. Yes, it takes a moment longer. But it is well worth it for the positive impression it creates. And yes, you risk hearing, "No, you may not." Accept that and either reprioritize things or take the caller's number and call back as quickly as possible. The caller who doesn't want to hold is not necessarily being pushy. Recently, a good friend of ours phoned her doctor's office. Because the receptionist knew her, she assumed she could just park her on hold with an "Oh, Nancy, hang on a minute" while she handled another call. That assumption was almost fatal. Nancy had just crawled to the phone after suffering a major medical problem.

Her case is a rare one, to be sure, but callers may have other legitimate reasons for not wanting, or not being able to hold. Remember that Knock Your Socks Off Service is delivered individually to match what each customer needs and expects.

Taking Messages

Good messages are accurate and complete. Be sure to get the caller's full name, company name and phone number. "Tell her Bill called" only works if the person the message is intended for knows only one Bill. To make sure you have the correct spelling of the caller's name and an accurate phone number, read it back. The date and time of the message is also important. Finally, be sure to put your own name on the message; if there is any question, the message recipient will be able to ask you for clarification.

Transferring Calls

Customers hate to be passed from pillar to post to Pammy to Paul and back again. Whenever possible, don't do it: Help the caller yourself or take a message and have the appropriate person return the call. When you do have to transfer a call, be sure to give the name and phone number of the person who will help them. This way, if there is any problem with the switch, the caller will be able to get back to the right person. And if you can, stay on the line to be sure the transfer goes smoothly.

> When you answer the phone, your store's image is on the line.
>
> —Headline
> *Video Business* magazine

17

Putting Pen to Paper

The writer who does the most gives his reader the most knowledge, and takes from him the least time.

—Charles Caleb Colton
Nineteenth-century English cleric

Verbal communication is quick and personal. It allows you to convey information and confirm immediate understanding while you observe the customer's body language and probe for additional questions or concerns. But verbal communication is not always possible.

Sometimes, written communication is required, or just is a good idea. You may not be able to reach the customer by phone or in person. You may need to send additional information. You may want to create a paper trail that can help both you and your customer track a service transaction that has spread out over several weeks or months. Even if there's no immediate need, a letter after a conversation with a customer can be a terrific way to confirm facts and details—not to mention to say thanks.

As with other aspects of Knock Your Socks Off Service, there are elements of style and substance that should be combined on your customer's behalf whenever you put pen to paper. While some of the written material your company sends to customers (from bills and advertising flyers to product documentation and legal notices) is necessarily standardized and impersonal, a more personal tone should come through in your own written communications.

Your Message

Why are you writing to your customer? Because you have something to say and a reason to say it:

• *You write to confirm understanding.* Suppose, for example, you're a travel agent. A couple wants your help in planning a winter vacation. They explain that they want to go to Colorado to ski, but don't want to stay at a big resort. They'd like to try to rent a condo—and it would be great if you could get one that was "no smoking." Having a spa and pool close by, as well as shopping, is important. And, of course, they want to get the cheapest possible package price.

It's a tall order. To fill it, you'll spend time discussing which of their requests are must-haves, and which are simply boy-it'd-be-great-if-we-coulds. But to show you're really on the ball, you follow up with a letter that outlines your discussion. The letter confirms the details for you both, and makes your customers feel like you really listened.

• *You write to create documentation.* A paper trail can confirm what action was or will be taken after the verbal conversation is over. It can serve as a quick summary of activity several months from now when your memory of the transaction has started to get a little fuzzy around the edges. It can even act as a contract, binding you and your customer to a particular agreement as to how to handle a given situation.

• *You write to solidify relationships.* Written communications are a way to make tangible (and memorable) the fleeting, transient nature of most service interactions. A thank-you note gives tangible evidence of your care and appreciation. An FYI or useful clipping from a current newspaper or magazine makes it clear you're thinking about your customers, even though you haven't seen them personally in a while. An "attaboy!" letter when something good happens to your customers (or their companies) says there's more than just money involved in the relationship.

EIGHT LETTER-WRITING TIPS

1. Whatever the content or purpose of your letter, make it neat and legible.
2. If you are writing on the record for your company, type or word-process your letter on company letterhead.
3. Unless you are sending a quick personal note, use standard 8½ by 11 paper. Smaller pages are more easily misplaced in filing; larger ones don't fit into the basic spaces of the modern office: in-baskets, file folders, copiers and faxes, and briefcases.
4. Get to the point quickly. State your purpose for writing in the first paragraph.
5. Be brief. Try to keep letters to one page whenever possible.
6. Write in the first person. *I* rather than *we*.
7. Write the way you speak. Your letter should sound as if it comes from a real person, not a bureaucrat.
8. Write right. Spell words correctly. Use proper style and grammar. If you're not sure, ask someone else to proofread for you and suggest ways to polish your prose.

Your Reader

Once you know why you are writing, consider who will be receiving your correspondence. What you know about your customer will help you set the tone of your letter and choose appropriate language. For example:

- Unless you are writing to someone who is very familiar with your business, avoid jargon and written shorthand; your customer may not know what a POS display or XD29 system is.
- Is your reader a child or an adult? Young or old? Is English his or her first language? Make sure your customers will understand what you write.
- What's the nature of your relationship at present? A satisfied customer will be puzzled by a letter that presumes a problem, while a disgruntled customer won't necessarily be overjoyed to learn you've introduced a new service or have a special offer running.

A cold, impersonal tone tells customers you're treating them like a number; too much jargon and legalese will confuse rather than confirm, irritating customers—or making them wonder if you have something to hide.

The Outcome

It should be clear from what you've written both why you've chosen to write and what, if anything, you expect your customers to do in response. Do they need to take any action? If so, by what date and in what form? Are they supposed to retain the correspondence for future reference? If so, for how long? Do they need to pass it along to someone else? If so, to whom and by when? Good writing is an extremely powerful part of good service. Inept writing undermines everything you've worked so hard to build.

Words fly, writings remain.

—Latin proverb

18

Exceptional Service Is in the Details

It is just the little touches after the average man would quit that make the master's fame.

—Orison Swett Marden
Founder, *Success* magazine

Asked about the difference between memorable and mundane buildings, Swiss architect Mies van der Rohe responded simply, "God is in the details, the details, the details." What's true of quality architecture is true of quality service: If you pay attention to the details, the right details, customers will know, and notice, and come back for more.

Everything Counts

The details surround us, no matter what kind of job we do. It's how we look, and how our workplace looks. It's how we speak and what we say. It's all the little extra courtesies and comforts we build into the service experience—or the myriad nagging annoyances we lose track of and make our customers wade through to do business with us.

Attention to details is a prime characteristic of high-performing organizations. From its earliest days, McDonald's

has made an organizational fetish of cleanliness. Crew kids
from the 1960s remember wielding brooms and dustpans to
clean up not only their own parking lot but the lots (sometimes
vacant) that bordered the restaurant. The daily refrain: "If
you've got time to lean, you've got time to clean."

⟶ A growing number of managers and executives today
understand that the example they set in turn sets a positive
tone for their organizations. For example:

- Fred Smith, the founder and chairman of Federal Express, begins many of his visits to FedEx facilities in far-
  flung cities by hopping on a typical delivery van.
- Bill Marriott, Jr., chairman of Marriott Hotels, often
  takes a turn at the hotel registration desk checking in
  guests; he also empties ashtrays in the lobby and picks
  up trash in the parking lot.
- And there isn't a manager at Walt Disney World or
  Disneyland who doesn't personally pick up, straighten,
  and worry after the thousand and one details that create
  an unparalleled experience for their customers.

These executives model attention to detail for their employees, just as you model it for customers and co-workers.

The Moments of Truth

Attention to detail is more than playing at or being a janitor. It
is the way you remember—and remind others—that contact
with any aspect of your work group gives your customers an
opportunity to form or revise their impressions, positive or
negative. At Scandinavian Airline System (SAS), employees
refer to their countless daily contacts with customers as Moments of Truth:

> ▲ A Moment of Truth occurs anytime a customer
> comes in contact with any part of your organization
> and uses that contact to judge the quality of the
> organization.

Anything and everything can become a Moment of Truth for your customers: the look of your store, building, or parking lot; the promises made in your advertising; how long your phone rings before being answered, and how the call is handled; written correspondence and bills . . . plus the memorable personal contacts your customers have with you.

Managing the Moments of Truth

When you began your current job, your orientation and training probably focused on the primary moments of truth built into your position. If you have been with your company for a long time, you've probably learned to recognize many more Moments of Truth that are important to your customers. To deliver true Knock Your Socks Off Service, you have to manage each and every Moment of Truth individually.

> **TIP:** The way that Moments of Truth are managed determines the grades customers give you on their mental report cards. Manage the moments well, and you receive A's and B's—and earn a repeat customer. Manage them poorly, and you earn D's and F's—and lose a customer in the bargain. Work to get good grades in this particular school and you'll find your diploma has cash value.

Over time, it's easy to think you've mastered all the various moments of truth your customers might present you with. Don't you believe it! No matter how experienced and skillful you become, you can always count on your customers to come up with something new. That's because customers can turn almost anything into a moment of truth.

To truly master the Moments of Truth in your services, develop these three customer-focused habits:

1. *Never stop learning.* The details that are important to your customers change from day to day as well as from customer to customer. There's always more to know.
2. *Ask your customers.* The only reliable way to identify

your customers' particular, peculiar moments of truth
is to get your customers to describe them to you.
3. *Ask your company.* In addition to your own informal,
day-to-day observations of customer preferences, your
company probably conducts continuing surveys and
studies. Make sure you know what the researchers
know that will help you serve your customers better.

It's not the tigers and bears that chase the customers away.
What bugs the customer the most are the mosquitoes and the
gnats—the little things. Jan Carlzon, SAS's CEO, summarizes
the SAS success story this way:

> We never started out to become 1,000 percent better at
> anything. Just one percent better at the thousand different
> things that are important to the customer. And it worked.

19

Good Selling
Is Good Service—
Good Service
Is Good Selling

Nothing happens until someone sells something.

—Marketing axiom

Sales and service are not separate functions. They are two sides of the same coin. Even if your title is "customer service representative" and a co-worker is a "sales associate," you both have the same ultimate goal: satisfying the customer. It wasn't always this way. In days gone by, sales and service personnel used to be adversaries:

- Sales and marketing people viewed their counter-parts in service and operations as "those guys who never want to help me make a sale and who screw it up after it's a done deal."

- Service and operations folk, for their part, tended to view sales and marketing people as "those people in suits who write outlandish ads, make ridiculous

promises to close a sale, and leave us holding the
bag with the customer."

The new attitude is that sales, marketing, service, and
operations all have the same goal: creating and retaining a
customer.

When Lines Overlap

Combining good selling and good service calls for some fi-
nesse. Consider the case of Edgar Pinchpenny III, the unhappy
owner of a Model 412-A Handy-Andy Cordless Electric Screwdriver. (You know he's unhappy because he is waving the 412-
A around, banging it on the desk and demanding his money
back.)

Using your very best Knock Your Socks Off Service skills
(listening—questioning—problem solving), you determine
that Pinchpenny is upset because the 412-A needs frequent
recharging and isn't very powerful. But you also know that the
412-A was built for small repair jobs around the house. It
absolutely was not designed for the industrial strength, barn-
building, automobile overhaul sort of work Pinchpenny is
trying to get out of it. That's why your company also sells the
much more expensive 412-C Turbo-Andy, the best professional power screwdriver in the industry and the perfect tool
for the job.

Now, tighten the chin strap on your thinking cap and
consider which of these four possible actions you would
recommend:

1. Tell Pinchpenny that if he hadn't been too cheap to
   buy the proper tools in the first place, he wouldn't be
   standing here screaming himself into a coronary.
2. Explain the limitations of the 412-A and the benefits
   of the 412-C to Pinchpenny, and recommend that he
   consider buying up.
3. Apologize to Pinchpenny for the inconvenience, explain the difference between the two models, offer to

personally make an exchange on the spot, and to give him a discount on the 412-C to compensate for being inconvenienced.

4. Apologize for the salesperson's stupidity, offer Pinchpenny an even exchange—the old, abused 412-A for a shiny new 412-C at no additional cost—throw in a free set of your best stainless steel screwdriver bits and offer to wash Pinchpenny's car.

We pick option 3 as the best course of action: It shows concern, responsiveness, and good salesmanship. Option 2 is a narrow, old-fashioned, service-as-complaint-department response. It isn't likely to keep Pinchpenny as a long-term customer. Options 1 and 4 are the kind of answers suitable for companies where frontline people are specifically recruited with IQs approximately equal to their shoe sizes.

When Selling Is Not Good Service

1. *No alternatives.* The customer's needs cannot be met by any product or service you offer, regardless of how well you can fix the problem, answer the question, or explain the current product or service.

2. *No slack.* You know how to solve the problem, but the customer came to you mad, has stayed mad and obviously wants to stay mad. There is very little chance to make the customer un-mad, let alone sell an upgrade or a switch to a different model.

3. *No point.* An upgrade or add-on would be totally illogical, unrelated, or inappropriate to the situation, as in, "Would you like some garlic bread to go with your cappuccino this morning?"

When Selling Is Good Service

1. *When the product or service the customer is using is wrong*—but you know which model, system or approach will better fit the customer's needs and are in a position to get it for the customer.

2. *When the product or service the customer acquired*

from your company is right—but some other part, piece, program, or process is needed before your product or service will perform properly: "Your computer operating system is Version 4.9. Our software is designed for the new 5.0 operating system. I do know of an upgrade for the 4.9 that might work."

3. *When the product or service in question is out of date*—"I can send you a new widget and walk you through the repair when you receive it. But I think it would be a good idea to consider a newer model that will do the job better. The Laser XJ7 has improved circuitry and can . . ."

4. *When an add-on feature will forestall other problems*—"I see you decided against extended warranty protection. But since you've had two problems during the warranty period, I wonder if you shouldn't reconsider that decision?"

5. *When changing the customer to a different product or service will be seen as value-added or TLC*—"This checking account requires a very high minimum balance. That's what caused the service charge you are concerned about. I'd like to recommend a different plan that I think will fit your needs better and save you from incurring future charges."

If it says CUSTOMER SERVICE on your name tag, then serving the customer is your full-time occupation. But remember: Even if nothing in your job description hints at a sales responsibility, you are a part of the sales and marketing team. Yours is always a two-hat job.

In reality, selling and service are inseparable.

—Leonard Berry, David Bennett, Carter Brown
Service Quality

20

Never Underestimate the Value of a Sincere Thank You

Thank You . . . Thank You, Thank You . . . and Thank *You*!!!

—Fozzie Bear

Remember when you were ten years old and what you wanted for your birthday was that electric train or special Barbie? And your grandmother gave you underwear instead. And your mom and dad stood there and looked at you and pinched you on the arm. "Now, what do you say?" they prompted. "Thank you, Grandma," you said. And your grandma beamed and patted you on the head.

Saying thank you is as important today as when your parents tried so hard to drum it into your head. In your job, you need to say thanks to your customers every day. You need to sincerely value the gift of business they bring you—even if it may not be as exciting as electric trains and Barbie dolls.

Nine Times When You Should Thank Customers

1. *When they do business with you . . . every time.* It bears repeating: Customers have options every time they need a service or product. It's easy to take regular

and walk-in customers for granted. Don't. Thank them for choosing to do business with you.

2. *When they compliment you (or your company).* Compliments can be embarrassing. But shrugging off customers' sincere praise says, "You dummy, I'm not really that good." Instead, accept it gracefully, say, "Thank you," and add, "I really appreciate your business."

3. *When they offer comments or suggestions.* Thanking customers for feedback says that you've heard what they had to say and value their opinion. Something as simple as "Thank you for taking the time to tell me that! It really helps us know where we can do better," delivered with eye contact and a smile, can work wonders.

4. *When they try a new product or service.* Trying something new can be uncomfortable. And risky. After all, the old and familiar is so, well, old and familiar. Thank customers for daring to try something different.

5. *When they recommend you to a friend.* When customers recommend you, they put themselves on the line. If you deliver, they look good. If you don't. . . . A written thank-you for a recommendation or a value-added token the next time you see those customers face-to-face says you value their recommendation.

6. *When they are patient . . . and not so patient.* Whether they tell you about it or not (and, boy, will some customers tell you about it!), no one likes to wait. Thanking customers for their patience says you noticed and value their time. It's also one of the quickest ways to defuse customers who have waited too long and are none too happy about it.

7. *When they help you to serve them better.* Some customers are always prepared. They have their account numbers right at their fingertips, always bring the right forms, and kept notes on their last service call. They make your life a lot easier; thank them for it.

8. *When they complain to you.* Thank them for complaining? Absolutely! Customers who tell you they are un-

happy are giving you a second chance. And that's quite a gift. Now you have a chance to win their renewed loyalty, which will give you additional opportunities to thank them in the future.

9. *When they make you smile.* A smile is one of the greatest gifts you can receive. Saying thank you just makes it better.

Three Ways to Say Thank You

1. *Verbally.* Say it after every encounter. And say it with feeling. "Thank-you-for-shopping-at-our-store," said like a freight train roaring past, doesn't impress customers. Make your thank you's warm, pleasant, and personal.
2. *In writing.* Send a follow-up note after a purchase or visit. Personalize it. Customers hate form letters. Write a thank you at the bottom of invoices or bills.
3. *With a gift.* Give something small, like a notepad or pen imprinted with your company name. It will help customers remember your business.

TIP: Make sure the value of the gift isn't out of balance with the nature of the business involved. Some customers worry that more expensive gifts may be an attempt to buy their business, rather than a token of appreciation.

Five Often-Forgotten Thank You's

1. *Your co-workers.* Give credit to those who help you. Thank co-workers whose concern for customers serves as a role model for you. Doing this in front of customers every chance you have tells customers they're dealing with a team effort.
2. *Your boss.* To make sure your managers give you the support you need, give positive feedback when they help you do your job.
3. *People in other departments of your company.* While you may be the one actually talking to the customers,

support people make the service you deliver possible. Thank them, either individually or as a group.

4. *Your vendors.* Without their professionalism, your customers wouldn't be receiving the satisfying service you're able to provide.

5. *You!* You do a tough job and deserve a pat on the back. Give yourself credit for a job well done. And take yourself out for an extra special reward once in a while.

TIP: The most effective thank you's are immediate, specific, sincere, and special.

Gratitude is not only the greatest virtue but the mother of all the rest.

—Cicero

The Problem-Solving Side of Knock Your Socks Off Service

Things don't always work out right. It's simply the law of averages. No matter how hard you try for perfection, sometimes you make a mistake. Sometimes your customer is wrong. And sometimes you just find yourself dealing with a difficult individual—someone who is never satisfied and tests your patience as well as your skills.

When things go wrong, it's time to play your trump card—your Knock Your Socks Off Service problem-solving skills. Being able to solve problems—to rescue the situation when it appears bleakest—is a key element in providing great service. It makes your job easier. It makes your company's business run smoother. And it's also a tremendous way to mend relationships with your customers and make them even more loyal.

21

Be a Fantastic Fixer

Customers don't expect you to be perfect. They do expect
you to fix things when they go wrong.

—Donald Porter
Senior Vice-President, British Airways

You go into a department store to buy a camcorder only to find
that the advertised model is sold out. You are disappointed—
even angry. *Why did they advertise it if they didn't have it!*
you ask yourself. However, one of the salespeople notices your
obvious upset. Maybe it's the expression on your face—or the
steam coming out of your ears.

Salesperson: May I help you?

You [*grumpily*]: I doubt it. I wanted an EZ-Use Camcorder,
but you people never have the stuff you advertise!

Salesperson: I'm sorry. We sold more than we expected
before the ad ran, so we only had a couple left this
morning. But we *are* offering a rain check, and we'll have
the EZ-Use back in stock in about four weeks.

You: Oh, great. Four weeks will be two weeks after my daugh-
ter's wedding. That's just dandy.

Salesperson: I can see that you are disappointed. It's frustrating to want something and then to learn that we don't
have it in stock. If you'll wait here for two minutes while
I check with my manager, I think I can help you today.

87

[*Two minutes later:*] Great news. I can offer you another manufacturer's comparable model for the same sale price. That way you can take your camcorder home today.
[*Beaming, and maybe slightly surprised, you leave the store with a new camcorder.*]

The Art of Service Recovery

The word *recovery* means to return to normal—to get things back in balance or good health. That's what the store's sales associate just did for the upset would-be camcorder buyer. In service, good recovery begins when you recognize (and the sooner the better) that a customer has a problem.

> **TIP:** Problems exist when individual customers say they do—anytime the customer feels upset, dismayed, angered, or disappointed. And what constitutes a disappointment for one customer is absolutely "no problem" for another. No matter, you can't wish (or order) a problem away because no reasonable person would be upset about that, or because it's not your fault, or it's not your company's fault, or even because the customer made a mistake.

Being a Fantastic Fixer, a real Knock Your Socks Off Service professional, involves taking thoughtful, positive actions that will lead disappointed customers back to a state of satisfaction with your organization. Healing injured customer feelings requires sensitivity to their needs, wants, and expectations.

The Recovery Process

Once a customer problem is identified, the service recovery process should begin. Not all of the six steps described below are needed for all customers. Use what you know about your company's products and services, and what you can discover about your customers' problems, to customize your actions to the specific situation. One size doesn't fit all.

1. *Apologize.* It doesn't matter who's at fault. Customers want someone to acknowledge that a problem occurred and show concern over their disappointment.
2. *Listen and empathize.* Treat your customers in a way that shows you care about them as well as about their problem. People have feelings and emotions. They want the personal side of the transaction acknowledged.
3. *Fix the problem quickly and fairly.* A "fair fix" is one that's delivered with a sense of professional concern. At the bottom line, customers want what they expected to receive in the first place, and the sooner the better.
4. *Offer atonement.* It's not uncommon for dissatisfied customers to feel injured or put out by a service breakdown. Often they will look to you to provide some value-added gesture that says, in a manner appropriate to the problem, "I want to make it up to you."
5. *Keep your promises.* Service recovery is needed because a customer believes a service promise has been broken. During the recovery process, you will often make new promises. When you do, be realistic about what you can and can't deliver.
6. *Follow up.* You can add a pleasant extra to the recovery sequence by following up a few hours, days, or weeks later to make sure things really were resolved to your customer's satisfaction. Don't assume you've fixed the person or the problem. Check to be sure.

TIP: Take immediate steps to solve problems. The sense of urgency you bring to problem solving tells your customers that recovery is every bit as important to you (and your organization) as the initial sale.

Asking for Trouble

Do we really need to even talk about when things go wrong? Why not just put our energy into doing it right the first time?

Because it won't always go right the first time. In fact, about a third of all the problems service providers have to deal with are caused by their customers. Service, even Knock Your Socks Off Service, involves human beings, and human beings are never 100 percent perfect. That's true for your customers, and it's true for you. Mistakes happen. We all know it. Even when you do your job correctly and satisfy the customer's need, a problem can occur if expectations are not met.

No matter what happens, or why, it is better to handle the occasional mishaps directly and effectively than to ignore them in hopes they'll go away, or to muddle through while hoping for the best.

Three Rules of Service Recovery

1. Do it right the first time.
2. Fix it if it fails.
3. Remember: There are no third chances.

—Dr. Leonard Berry
Researcher, Texas A&M University

22

Use the Well-Placed "I'm Sorry"

A few words of regret is a way of saying you care, a show of sensitivity to the ragged edges of another's emotion.

—Robert Conklin
How to Get People to Do Things

The words are so simple—"I'm sorry"—yet we hear them far too infrequently. In fact, our research shows that when customers tell a company about a problem with a product or service, they receive an apology less than half the time. That's about half as often as they should. The solution to every problem, whether major or minor, should start with a sincere apology.

Why is it so hard for us to say "I'm sorry" to our customers? First and foremost, we may be intimidated by the words. We may think that "I'm sorry" says "I've failed," "I'm not a good person," or "I'm not professional." Nothing could be further from the truth. An apology is simply an acknowledgement that things aren't going right in your customer's eyes.

Legal Jeopardy

Today, there is also a tendency to equate being sorry with an admission of personal or corporate liability, that being sorry means that you are somehow to blame. Megabuck lawsuits are common stories from the six o'clock news to prime-time entertainment programs. It's understandable that companies worry about the potential financial consequences of an apology and individuals are reluctant to take the blame personally.

If your job has legal or regulatory aspects, make sure you understand what they are and how they affect what you do. But don't assume that you're not allowed to say, "I'm sorry you were inconvenienced," when the inevitable snafu occurs. Actually, a sincere apology, delivered in a timely and professional manner, often goes a long way toward heading off potential legal problems. When you show your willingness to make sure your customers receive what they expect to receive, you relieve them of the need to even think about starting a fight.

Customer Jeopardy

Just as apologizing is not an admission of responsibility ("I'm sorry *we* did this to you"), neither is it an opportunity to place blame ("I'm sorry *you* were too stupid to read the directions before turning it on and shorting it out").

We all know that customers don't always use their own common sense or the painstakingly detailed directions we

give them. Sometimes, for whatever the reason, they do it wrong—with predictably disastrous consequences. Then they look to us to fix it. And since no one likes to admit a mistake, they'll often blame us in the process.

> **TIP:** Tempting as it may be, resist the urge to rap them over the nose as you would a naughty puppy. A sincere apology is a personal and professional acknowledgment that your customer was disappointed or inconvenienced. It really doesn't matter who—or what—was at fault.

When Vision Cable of Charlotte, North Carolina, was hit hard by Hurricane Hugo a few years ago, thousands of customers lost cable service. Vision Cable employees did everything they could to restore service as quickly as possible. Crews worked day and night. But general manager Milton Moore also personally apologized to customers in a series of radio ads, assuring them they would receive credit for every day they were without service and asking for their help in reporting any additional service interruptions.

Did he have to do that? Of course not. But his customers heard the message loud and clear: Let's all get things back to normal as quickly as we can. If Moore can apologize for a hurricane, just think how much you can accomplish with a well-placed, "I'm sorry."

Scapegoating

When things go wrong, there's an almost instinctive urge to direct the customer's attention elsewhere: "If those 'smart guys' in computer services could ever figure out how to make this system work the way it's supposed to, we wouldn't have to put you through long waits like this," or "Maintenance was supposed to clean that up last night, but I guess they were too busy taking a coffee break. So you ended up stepping in it."

> **TIP:** Scapegoating another part of your organization for a service breakdown simply tells your customers that you're

separate departments working in isolated and even ad-versarial ways instead of a tight-knit team working for them. Don't do it—not to each other, not to yourself.

Do It Right

A vague apology delivered in an impersonal, machinelike manner, can be worse than no apology at all. Effective apologies are:

1. *Sincere.* While you may not know exactly what your customers are feeling and experiencing individually, the way the employees of Vision Cable did, you can be genuine in your concern.
2. *Personal.* Apologies are far more powerful when they are delivered in the first person: "I am sorry that you are experiencing a problem." Remember that to the customer, you—not some mysterious we or they—are the company.
3. *Timely.* Don't wait to find out why there is a problem or what caused it before expressing regret that the problem exists in the first place. The sooner you react to a distressed customer, the better.

I believe that if you are honest and straightforward with customers, they will treat you like a neighbor when circumstances beyond your control put you in a "one-down" position.

—Milton Moore
General Manager, Vision Cable

23

Fix the Person

Here's your food and I hope you choke on it!!

—Fast-food server to a customer
who complained about waiting ten
minutes to be served. [*It's true.
We're not making it up.*]

The toughest part of dealing with people, as you already know, is dealing with people. When products develop problems, customers have an object to cuss out, kick, yell at, and focus their feelings on. When a service breaks down, on the other hand, the focus of their emotional reaction is on you.

It is tempting to respond in kind to the emotional fireworks set off by disgruntled customers. Tempting, but not very wise, and certainly not very productive. Meeting anger with anger, sarcasm with sarcasm, frustration with impatience, or ignoring the emotional element altogether, leaves both server and served feeling badly bruised. And understandably, neither may be anxious for a repeat performance. Knock Your Socks Off Service professionals recognize the emotional element of a service breakdown, and manage the recovery in a calm, professional, even-tempered way. To do that, it's not enough to just fix the problem. You also have to fix the person.

Color-Coding Your Response

Just as problems will have different solutions, fixing the person takes a different form depending on the "color" of your customer's emotional state. As a service professional, you've probably encountered it all, from coldly angry to virtually frothing at the mouth. Some people seem very understanding when things go wrong, some make you feel absolutely terrible for playing a role in a service snafu, and others can instill a very real sense of fear in you.

We find it helpful to group customers by their reactions into three emotional colors: Blasé Blue, Ornery Orange, and Raging Red.

• *Blasé Blue customers.* These customers don't give you enough emotional clues to decipher their level of upset. For some, the service breakdown may simply be a nonemotional event—they roll with the punch and don't let it bother them. But be aware that seemingly neutral customers can move up the emotional scale if you don't take them seriously.

• *Ornery Orange customers.* Annoyed, these people exhibit mild irritation because their experience has fallen short of their expectations. Take them lightly or refuse to acknowledge their upset, however, and you can quickly escalate them to four-alarm fire status.

• *Raging Red customers.* These customers have major feelings of ire and frustration; they feel victimized and hurt by the service breakdown. Usually you won't have any trouble identifying their level of concern—it will be obvious to everyone within a three-block radius.

To see the differences among the three, consider these reactions to essentially the same initial situation:

Blasé Blue:	Bob's flight arrives one hour late, but he had a ninety-minute layover and can still make his next connection, so Bob's plans haven't been affected.
Ornery Orange:	Olivia's flight is one hour late, causing her to miss a connection and to have to re-book on a later flight.

Raging Red: Ray's flight is one hour late, causing him
                         to miss the last connection, resulting in
                         an unplanned overnight stay and the
                         need to call and reschedule a full day's
                         worth of appointments.

Knowing the emotional color of your customer will help you choose the best people-fixing techniques. Here's a handy guide. If your customer is:

Blasé Blue	Ornery Orange	Raging Red
• Show surprise.	• Show urgency.	• Show empathy.
• Use general people-handling skills.	• Enlist the customer in generating solutions.	• Allow venting.
		• Create calm.
• Key into the customer.	• Create added value.	• Listen actively.
		• Plan follow-up.

Tip of the Iceberg

Fixing the person is an important element of a well-conceived recovery effort because many times a customer's emotional reaction is only tangentially tied to the real service problem. When you encounter an upset customer, you can't tell from the initial emotional readout whether their problem stems from a late flight, a broken radiator, a bounced check, or even, well . . . consider this illustration:

A friend of ours spent some years working behind the counter of an ice cream store. One very busy day, a business-man came in and ordered a banana split. She made it, handed it to him, and went on to the next customer. Moments later, the customer was back. "This banana split has no bananas!" he hollered. "What kind of a moron makes a banana split with no bananas!!"

Stunned by the outburst, our friend could do little more than look at the man—and at the banana-less split. When he finally paused for a breath, she made the necessary effort:

"Gee, I'm awfully sorry about that. No bananas is a pretty serious offense in a banana split. I think I'd be upset, too. Please, let me make you a fresh one—and refund your money."

About that time, the customer became aware that he was ranting and raving over a bowl of ice cream, under the stares of the other customers and confronted by nothing more threatening than the sincere concern on a young woman's face. He started laughing. And she started to smile. And the other customers started to giggle and laugh. The upshot was that while she was making the new banana split, he apologized to her. And, perhaps needless to say, became a regular at that ice cream shop.

> When a service tech goes on site, he has two repairs: He has to fix the equipment and fix the customer. And fixing the customer is more important.
>
> —Bill Bleuel
> Customer Satisfaction Consultant and
> Professor of Quantitative Methods,
> Pepperdine University

24

Fair Fix the Problem

If you have trouble, it reduces the likelihood that the person is going to buy the next time.

—Joseph M. Juran
Founding father of Quality Control

Have you noticed that some people just seem naturally good at problem solving? No matter what the situation, no matter what the conflict, they are always able to see some course of action that will get the job done. Perhaps you are one of those people.

If you aren't, you may think, "I'll never be able to be as effective as they are—I don't have the talent." Wrong. Problem-solving is a skill, not a talent. Effective problem solvers have simply learned to use their skills. To practice and hone your problem-solving skills, we recommend using a three-step framework: Listen—Probe—Solve.

Step 1: LISTEN to Find the Problem

The importance of good listening cannot be overstated. In a problem-solving situation, you are listening for two reasons:

1. To allow your customers to vent their frustration or irritation—part of the "fix the person" process; and

2. To find the real problem (which may be obvious, but sometimes isn't).

For example, "listen" to this customer's complaint:

"I bought a Kid-Pro Bike from you people last night. The box must have weighed eighty pounds! I finally got it into my car—no help from you guys—and home, and it took me an hour to get it out of the car, into the house and open. I mean really! This is a kid's bike and you need Arnold Schwarzenegger to open the box! And after all that, the directions were missing!! How am I supposed to put it together without the directions!?!"

Upset customers are apt to bring multiple issues into their tirade. It's important to this customer that she had difficulty leaving the store, getting the box from her car to the house, and opening the box. But the real problem is the missing directions.

> **TIP:** Don't interrupt as soon as you think you've heard the problem. You may be right, but you may not be. Listen until your customers are done explaining. They'll feel better for getting the whole story off their chest, and you may discover pieces of the puzzle you didn't even know were missing. (Your customers have been practicing their little speech all the way to your store or office—don't deprive them of the right to deliver it, and as dramatically or passionately as they like.)

Step 2: PROBE for Understanding and Confirmation

Customers, particularly upset customers, don't always explain everything clearly or completely. Ask questions about anything you may not understand or need clarified. Then, when you feel you have identified and clearly understand the problem, repeat it back to the customer.

> "I'm sorry you are experiencing some frustration with the Kid-Pro Bike you purchased. As I understand it, you have the bike at home in pieces with no directions to tell you how to put it together. That would frustrate me, too."

> **TIP:** Use this step to make it clear that you agree that what the customer says is a problem really is a problem. Nothing annoys customers more than to hear a service representative respond to their concerns with an offhand "So?"

STEP 3: Find and Implement SOLUTIONS

If the problem is one that you have encountered before, you may already know the best solution. In that case, use the "feel, felt, found" approach to present it:

> "I can understand that you feel _____. Other people, including myself, have felt the same way. We've found that _____ solves the problem."

When the best solution is less obvious, present several options and ask for the customer's preferences.

> "I could have someone check in the stockroom to see if we have another carton with a set of instructions in it. Or, if you're in more of a hurry, I could run a copy of the master copy we have. But maybe you just want to take a look at the Kid-Pro model we have set up here and then call me as you're putting yours together if you have any questions."

Involving customers in generating solutions not only starts to rebuild the relationship, it gives them the feeling that your business really is interested in satisfying their needs. You'll find that most customers bring a sense of fair play with them and will often expect far less than you'd think. In our research into telephone repair services, for example, we learned that customers who experienced problems on the weekend didn't expect immediate service. They reasoned that telephone repair technicians wanted to spend weekend time with their own families, just like customers.

> **TIP:** If the solution you suggest is rejected by your customer, or is met with a lukewarm reception, you may not be solving the real problem. Keep probing by asking what else your customer would like to see happen.

One Extra Step

Sometimes, solving the actual problem is not quite enough. Remember that the purpose of a Fantastic Fix isn't only to correct the problem, but also—perhaps more importantly—to keep the customer. Rebuilding a damaged relationship, particularly when a customer feels victimized by the service breakdown, may require taking an extra step we call "symbolic atonement." It means making an appropriate gesture that says, "I want to make it up to you." Atonement is a way of providing a value-added touch to tell customers their business is important to you.

> "I'm glad you gave us a chance to make things right. Before you leave, let me write our store phone number and my home phone number on the directions. And since you had to make an extra trip, I'd like to give you one of these personalized bike license plates. What's your son's name?"

Don't fight, make it right.

—Hardee's complaint-handling policy

25

All Rules Were Meant to Be Broken

(Including This One)

The exception proves the rule.

—Seventeenth century proverb

Rules are everywhere. We encounter formal rules in the form of laws and policies—"No right turn on red," or, "Returns must be accompanied by receipt." Other rules are informal, taught by custom or experience—"When you bump into another person, say 'Excuse me,'" or, "Allow extra time when driving during rush hour."

Rules should share a single purpose: to make life run more smoothly, more efficiently, in a more organized and orderly fashion. We sometimes call this purpose the "spirit" of the law. But rules don't always fulfill their spirit. In fact, sometimes they work against what we're trying to accomplish. That's why it's important for Knock Your Socks Off Service professionals to understand the rules that direct their efforts.

Rules vs. Assumptions

We are so used to rules in our lives that sometimes, when we don't know the answer or aren't comfortable making a decision of our own, we're tempted to make up a rule to fill the gap. Or, in the stress of the moment, we may borrow a rule from another setting that seems to fit our current situation.

For example, imagine you're a new cashier. A customer comes in and asks to write a check for $20 more than the amount of purchase. You don't know what your store policy is, and there's no one nearby to ask. What do you do?

- You might assume that cashing checks for over the amount is against the rules and say no.
- Or you may borrow a rule from your last job and allow the customer to write the check for $5 or $10 more.

Either option is tempting because it puts you in control of the situation and keeps you from having to say, "Gee, I don't know if you can do that." But not knowing all the rules is natural! In fact, not knowing and finding out—for yourself and for the customer—is one of the best ways to learn on the job. Instead of assuming there must be a rule that will make you say no, find out how to say yes.

Our good friend, service consultant Dick Schaaf, recalls that as a McDonald's crew kid some twenty years ago, he'd occasionally encounter a customer who wanted a grilled-cheese sandwich. While grilled cheese wasn't on the official menu, the restaurant did have the essential ingredients: a grill,

bread (buns), and cheese. So, instead of saying no to the request, his restaurant said yes.

Nowadays, he's prone to wander into any fast-food outlet he finds and place a similar order. Sadly, he usually faces frontline employees who don't feel empowered to grant his off-the-wall request, and managers who will often go to absurd lengths to say no, invoking invisible company rules, local health codes, even state laws that supposedly govern (or forbid) the making of grilled-cheese sandwiches!

Red Rules vs. Blue Rules

Rules are important when they protect the public safety or reflect experience that says dire consequences will occur if the wrong things happen. But other rules are simply habits and customs with hardened arteries—systems that grow inflexible with age and take on a rigidity never intended.

In healthcare, some organizations work in terms of Red rules and Blue rules: *Red rules* are rules that cannot be broken. They are there to protect the life or well-being of the patient—for example, NO SMOKING WHERE HIGHLY COMBUSTIBLE OXYGEN IS IN USE. *Blue rules* are designed to make the hospital experience run more smoothly for patient and staff alike—for example, INCOMING PATIENTS ARE PROCESSED THROUGH THE ADMITTING DEPARTMENT.

Healthcare workers have to know when a Blue rule, such as FILL OUT THE ADMISSION FORMS FIRST, should or must be broken; in the Emergency Room, or when a pregnant woman arrives in labor, the paperwork can wait.

Do you know the Red rules and the Blue rules in your company? Red rules may be set by the government in the form of laws or regulations, or by your company's management. Blue rules may evolve from department policy or past experience. You need to understand which is which case and be able to explain the rules to your customers so they, in turn, know why you're doing what you're doing.

TIP: If it's a Red rule, usually it will take precedence over the customer's wishes.

> "I'm sorry that you find the seat belts in your car uncomfortable. But because of your safety, it is against the law for me to remove them. Perhaps we can make an adjustment that will make them fit more comfortably."

If it's a Blue rule, usually you can find a way to flex the letter of the law but keep the spirit.

> "There's no pay phone here, and this one is intended for internal use, but you can dial 9 for an outside line if you need to call to let your babysitter know you're running a little late."

Breaking vs. Bending the Rules

Know your own limits. If you believe an exception should be made, but aren't sure you can or should do it, ask a more experienced peer, your supervisor, or your manager.

Without formal and informal rules, service would become chaotic— and customers would never know what to expect. Just because you think that breaking or bending a rule won't cause the ceiling to fall doesn't mean you should take it lightly. Know the nature of the rule in question, the reason for the rule, the consequences of not following it, then help your customer make the system work.

> Rules exist to serve, not enslave.
>
> —Software programmer's axiom

26

Customers From Hell . . . Are Customers Too

There are no "bad" customers; some are just harder to please than others.

—Someone who never waited on a customer in his or her life

There is a world of difference between keeping your composure while working with an upset, angry customer who has had a bad day in consumerland and the burning sensation you get in your stomach when you come face-to-face with a fire-breathing, show-no-mercy, take-no-prisoners Customer From Hell.

Customers who have been *through* consumer hell need your help, support, and understanding. Those who come to you direct *from* hell need the special care and handling you might give a live hand grenade or an angry rattlesnake.

You would never tell the second group to their faces what you're thinking—"Arrrggghhh, another Customer From Hell"—but there's nothing wrong with admitting to yourself that this is what working with them feels like.

Customers From Hell play a simple game. Their goal is to

get under your skin, to provoke you to counterattack. They taunt; you react; they win. If you lose control, you lose everything. Often, your first impulse is either to run and hide or to smack 'em. Or both. But you can't really do either. So, what do you do?

First, develop some perspective. Customers From Hell are relatively few and far between (unless your company is going out of its way to cheat or provoke normally pleasant people). Most of your customers want to deal with you in a cheerful, positive way. And even the really bad ones are still customers.

Second, remember that you are a pro. You know your job and your company. You know your products and how they perform. And *you* know how to handle people, even when it's the end of the day, the end of the week, or the end of August and the air-conditioning is broken.

Third, be a master of the art of calm. Let the upset and anger wash over you without sticking. Angry customers are almost never mad at you personally. They are mad at a situation they don't like.

Two Approaches to Obnoxious Customers

1. *See no evil, hear no evil.* If you start thinking of customers as jerks and idiots, before you know it, you'll start treating them as badly as they treat you. Worse yet, you will start to treat the innocent like the guilty.

Mr. John Q. McNasty of the ABC Widget Company is the biggest jerk you have ever had to deal with. One day, you decide to fight fire with fire and be just as rude and insulting as he is. You give him a dose of his own medicine—and you feel great. John Q., of course, goes back to ABC and tells everyone what a stinker you are, that all *he* did was ask for a little service. Soon you begin to notice other ABC people acting up when you deal with them. And then, of course, you have to show these jerks that you can be just as tough as they are. And then. . . . You get the point, right?

Customers From Hell feed on your reactions. They use a nasty response to justify their own nasty behavior. Ignoring their rude and crude words and actions sends the message,

"Slam, bang, and cuss all you want. I am not intimidated." And that message—demonstrated, but not spoken—gives *you* the advantage.

> **TIP:** Don't try your company's Ten Commandments on Customers From Hell. Quoting rules or policy to justify your actions simply gives this kind of person something concrete to scream about.

2. *Draw a line in the sand.* There are some things a service person is *never* obligated to take from customers:
   • *Profanity:* If you are personally offended, shocked or dismayed by foul language, you have a right to deal with it. Carol D. McNasty calls to inquire about a billing problem. Along the way she "loses it" and starts cursing like a stevedore. If her language is a barrier to your being able to solve her problem, say so. Politely, of course:

> "Excuse me. I can't help you if you insist on using that sort of language. If you continue, I am going to hang up."

Then do it. Then go immediately to your manager and explain what you did and why. More often than not (some say 80 percent of the time), Ms. McNasty will call back, apologize, and ask to start over again. And that should end the incident.
   • *Physical Abuse:* Unless you are running a mud wrestling arena, a customer never has the right to touch you. There is a legal name for being touched, jostled, pushed, shoved, or threatened with physical acts by a customer: assault and battery. "That's just the way some customers are—they don't mean any harm," is not an excuse.
   You are assistant maître d' at Chez Hot Stuff Café, the smartest, trendiest new restaurant in town. You are booked solid for the evening when the McNastys arrive with three friends and no reservation. Mr. McN. takes you by the arm, leads you aside, and tells you that you *will* seat his party immediately if you know what's good for

you. All the time he is talking, he is smiling—and squeez-ing your upper arm in an obviously menacing way. Make positive eye contact, smile right back and say, "If you do not stop twisting my arm immediately, I will call Secur-ity." If he stops, offer to put him on the waiting list. If not, call for your manager in a firm, *loud* voice. Then call 911.

Which Tactic Is Best?

Both approaches can be correct in the right situation. Care, calm, and kid-glove handling can quiet the savage in the most beastly customer—most of the time. But there are times when drawing a line is important. Some behavior is just plain out of bounds.

Look for the gifts—the things that every unpleasant en-counter can teach you about dealing with ugly human behavior.

—Rebecca Morgan
Morgan Seminar Group

Knock Your Socks Off Service Fitness:

Taking Care of *You*

We've focused our attention primarily on the customer. But there's another important player in the service game: you. A savvy service professional learns that self-management is every bit as important as managing the customer's experience.

Providing Knock Your Socks Off Service shouldn't be an impossible quest—or a personal ordeal. Like an athlete constantly in training, or a musician perfecting an instrument, you need to develop, evaluate, pace and manage yourself as well as your performance. That means work, but it also means celebrating a job well done.

How you feel about yourself and the job you are doing—whether you love it or are overwhelmed by it—will inevitably be reflected in the quality of your work. Knock Your Socks Off Service should be rewarding for *everyone* involved.

27

Master the Art of Calm

The stress puzzle is the mind-body link: What roles do our emotions, thoughts, and perceptions play in the way we experience and physically respond to stressful situations?

—Dr. Frances Meritt Stern
President, Institute of Behavioral Awareness

You're not any good to anyone when you are stressed up, stressed out, overwrought, anxious, moody, belligerent, nasty, and still waiting for that first cup of coffee. The emotional labor involved in modern service jobs can actually be more draining than lifting boxes or pouring concrete. All the good stuff built into your job will never be enough if you don't learn how to cope with and counteract the stress.

In theme parks from Disneyland and Walt Disney World to Knott's Berry Farm, Opryland and Carowinds, people at the frontlines are taught the concepts of onstage and offstage.

- *Onstage* is anywhere a customer can see or hear you.

- *Offstage* is everywhere else, safely away from the public eye.

An employee who is feeling stressed can ask a supervisor to take over the ride operation, concession stand, or broom so they can get themselves back together. Once offstage, they can let their emotions out, deal with them, put their game face back on, and come back to the job without worrying about putting their next customer through the third degree.

You, your manager, and your organization have to work together to manage the environment in which you work. But only you can manage the way you react to a given service encounter. How do you cope? There are any number of techniques for reducing stress, whether inside your cubicle or out on the sales floor. Find those that work best for you and practice them every day. Here are ten to get you started.

Ten Stress Reducers

1. *Breathe.* Deep breathing is one of the oldest stress-busting techniques, and one of the best. Stress can upset the normal balance of oxygen and carbon dioxide in your lungs. Deep breathing corrects this imbalance and can help you control panic thinking. Take a deep breath through your nose—hold it for seven seconds (no more)—then let it out slowly through your mouth. Do this three to six times.

2. *Smile.* You make your mood, and your mood can stress or relax you. Smiling is contagious. When you see a customer looking a little glum, make eye contact and turn on one of your best and brightest. Ninety-nine times out of a hundred, you'll get a smile right back.

3. *Laugh.* Maintaining a sense of humor is your best defense against stress. Stress psychologist Frances Meritt Stern tells of a difficult client she had been dealing with for years. "That clown is driving me up a wall!" she often complained. One day, she began to envision him complete with white-face, floppy shoes, and a wide, foolish grin. With this picture tickling her funny bone, she was able to manage her stress response and focus on doing her job.

4. *Let it out.* Keep your anger and frustration locked up inside and you are sure to show it on the outside. Instead,

make an appointment with yourself to think about a particularly stressful customer later—and then keep the appointment. Unacknowledged tension will eat you up, but delaying your reaction to stress-causing events can be constructive. It puts you in control.

> **TIP:** To get extra value from the technique, service representative Amy Gruber keeps a stress log of her most frustrating customers and situations. Adding an entry to the log helps calm her, and over several years the log has become a guide to dealing with her stress load.

5. *Take a one-minute vacation.* John Rondell, a sales consultant, has a vivid image of himself snorkeling off a beautiful white-sand beach in the Caribbean. He has worked on the scene until he can experience being there and lose all sense of time and place, even though his visits last only a minute or two. Now he can return to his "favorite place" following a stressful call or before talking to a stress-inducing customer.

6. *Relax.* We tend to hold in tension by tightening our muscles. Instead, try isometrics: tensing and relaxing specific muscles or muscle groups. Make a fist, then relax it. Tighten your stomach muscles, then relax them. Push your palms against each other, then relax your arms. Some people get so good at it, they can do their exercises right under the customer's nose.

7. *Do desk aerobics.* Exercise is a vital component of a stress-managed life. Try these two "desk-er-cizes":

- While sitting at your desk, raise your feet until your legs are almost parallel to the floor. Hold them there, then let them down. Do this five times.
- Rotate your head forward and from side to side (but not back—that can strain rather than stretch). Roll your shoulders forward and then lift them up and back. This feels especially good after you've been sitting or standing for some time.

8. *Organize.* Organizing gives you a sense of control and lessens your stress level. "I organize the top of my desk whenever I am waiting on hold," says Eric Johnson, a telephone customer service representative. "Before I leave for the day, I make sure everything is put away, and that I have a list of priorities made out for the next day."

9. *Talk positive.* Vent your anger and frustration in positive ways. Sharing customer encounters with co-workers helps you find the humor in the situation and gain new ideas for handling similar situations. But constant negative talk that rehashes old ground will only re-create and reinforce, not diminish, your stress.

10. *Take a health break.* Make your normal breaks into stress breaks. Consider walking outside, reading a chapter from a favorite book, or just sitting with your eyes closed for a few minutes. Bring healthy snacks and juice to work to substitute for the standard coffee and donuts.

To paraphrase: You only serve as good as you feel. You need to take care of yourself. And you are the only one who can.

> When your customer is the most anxious, you need to be at your best—most competent, confident, calmest, and in control of yourself.

> —Chip R. Bell

28

Keep It Professional

Customers are our best friends.

—Sign on a company wall

Today, it's common to hear executives and managers proclaim, "Customers are our best friends." But Knock Your Socks Off Service professionals know that, for all the light banter and personal fanfare, there's a critical difference between being friendly and having a friendship.

- ▲ *A friendly transaction* is a clear and understandable goal in any business—treating customers courteously, attentively, and professionally mimics the "transactional treatment" we would give to a close personal friend (and, in doing so, greases the wheels of commerce).

- ▲ *A friendship,* on the other hand, is a relationship that begins and continues outside the bounds of the work we do and involves personal commitments far beyond the scope of the normal customer/server interactions.

Does that mean that customers should never be friends, or that friends shouldn't be customers? Of course not. We all hope our friends will chose to do business with us, and it's not unusual—and typically quite a compliment—when business relationships grow into interesting friendships.

If the letters to advice columnists are to be believed, it seems that a good percentage of today's romantic relationships grow out of service professionals meeting customers. But that's the result of a relationship that continues off the job.

Taking Care of Business

On the job, your customers are customers first and foremost: They have come to you not for conversation and companionship, but because they are trying to get their needs met through the business that employs you. Your customers need your help as a service professional, be it to ring up a sale, create a new hairstyle, or deliver 500 pounds of industrial adhesive. They aren't there to look for a new friend.

> **TIP:** You are the most helpful when you remain professional, but with a personal touch. That means not confusing your off-the-job personal friendships with on-the-job, friendly, professional transactions.

It's worth noting that friendships can suffer some bruises when business gets in the way. Do your friends feel secure enough in your friendship to risk your displeasure if your friendly business services aren't satisfying? Even friends of long standing may feel uncomfortable being honest with you in a business relationship that seems more a friendship than a professional partnership. They may withhold pointed feedback or suppress complaints, and ultimately may even take their business elsewhere, rather than create hurt feelings by telling you about their dissatisfaction.

Appearances also have an effect, both on customers who don't know you as well and on supervisors and co-workers who do.

- The next person in line may be made distinctly uncomfortable by the personal chatter and other evidences of a relationship that excludes them. Even though they may not be waiting any longer than normal, that wait will "feel" longer to them if they think you could get to their needs more quickly by dispensing with what may appear to them to be idle chit-chat.

- Your co-workers and managers may have a similar reaction if they think you're giving unequal or preferential treatment to one particular customer, especially if there are others nearby to wait and watch.

Remember that a Moment of Truth for you and your business involves any time your customer has an opportunity to observe what you do and make a judgment on the quality involved. The best rule of thumb is to "keep it professional" at all times.

Involvement Varies

The difference between friendly and friendship and the difference between empathy and sympathy are related. When your friends experience pain or joy, you share those feelings with them. In that context, you sympathize as part of your friendship. When friends are in trouble, you may even offer advice. But it is not your role to fix everything for them.

When customers are upset, they expect you to care, too. But they also expect you to do something else that has nothing to do with a personal relationship: to fix their problem, to make things right, without becoming personally involved.

Showing empathy as part of being professionally friendly is the best way to respect the difference between personal and professional conduct.

Who You Are vs. What You Do

There's another personal relationship that often gets over-looked by service professionals concentrating on doing their jobs to the best of their abilities: the one between you and those closest to you—your family and loved ones. During the course of the business day, you'll have many experiences and encounters—plenty of answers to the innocent question, "And how was your day, dear?" But while the stories you share can help your family better understand why you care so much about the work you do, it's unfair to overburden them with your professional concerns, just as it's unprofessional to violate the confidences of your customers.

> **TIP:** Draw a clear line between who you are and what you do—who you are goes home with you at the end of the day; what you do stays at work.

When it gets dark, I go home.

> —Author Ray Bradbury [explaining to an interviewer why there were no light fixtures in his office]

29

Party Hearty

You deserve a break today!

—McDonald's jingle

It's true. You do deserve a break today—and every day! It's important to take time out to celebrate your successes. Be good to yourself for doing a terrific job. No one else can celebrate as well as you can because no one else knows how well you've done.

If you've ever—and who hasn't?—spent an hour or ten complaining about stupid customers or unsolvable problems, remember the FCC rule of equal time. Spend as much time, or better yet, more time, rehashing successes. From time to time, go out with your colleagues and celebrate each other for surviving and thriving in the work you do. Is it bragging about yourself? Sure. But there's no reason to downplay your skills and accomplishments. And recognizing your successes today will help motivate you to come back for more tomorrow.

Learning to Celebrate

Some people seem born knowing how to give themselves, and the people around them, needed pats on the back for work well done. But for most of us, celebrating ourselves doesn't come easy. We get so embarrassed when others start to sing our praises, we wouldn't even think of jumping in with a verse or two of our own. That's an attitude Knock Your Socks Off Service professionals can—and should—learn to leave behind. Give yourself permission to be terrific. That's right: You need to make a conscious decision to allow yourself to occasionally revel in doing well. Once you do, we guarantee you'll learn to love the habit.

Still think it will be hard to get the hang of this positive feedback thing? Then start by practicing on someone else. Thank a colleague for helping you out. Make a point of letting your supervisor know something good about a co-worker. Pass along a tip or trick you've learned from someone else—and make it clear who taught it to you.

Notice that the examples above have a common element: They focus attention first on an action or accomplishment, then on the individual or team of individuals involved. In other words, you're not glowing all over someone just for being a wonderful person. Rather, you're taking note of what they did and why it was so terrific. Now start doing the same thing for yourself.

Five Ways to Celebrate

There are countless ways to observe and have some fun with your service successes. We've listed our five favorite ways

below just to get you started. Good celebration has one under-lying tenet: You don't build someone up by tearing someone else down. Never celebrate one person's service performance by demeaning another's.

Remember Doctor Seuss' *Yertle the Turtle*? He tried to celebrate his own worth by rising high on the backs of his fellow turtles. It worked for a while, but eventually Yertle met the fate shared by all who lift themselves up by putting others down: He ended up face-first in the mud. Standing tall on the merits of your own service successes means celebrating personal victories, but it also means seeking out and celebrating the victories of your co-workers as well. Try these five:

1. *Take yourself out to lunch.* Treat yourself to a special lunch or dinner or even breakfast. Invite a friend or co-worker (or several) to go along and—this is the important part—make sure they know exactly what you are celebrating and why.

2. *Take a co-worker out to lunch.* This one works the same as the one above, only this time the reason for celebration is a good service performance that has inspired you or given you added satisfaction or motivation in your job. Involving several others reinforces the teamwork and camaraderie that makes good service organizations something special to be a part of.

3. *Buy balloons or flowers or something fun.* A balloon or fresh-cut flower on your desk can symbolize a recent service achievement. It also brightens up your work space and lets other people know you're feeling good about something. When they ask you, you'll have a chance to explain, which will make you feel even better.

> **TIP:** Consider giving the impromptu award you've presented yourself "legs": Enjoy it on your desk for a day, then pass it on to a co-worker who just handled a Customer From Hell with grace and aplomb.

4. *Make a "brag sheet."* When you spend a lot of time working on the skills you would like to improve, it's easy to forget to celebrate the strengths you already have. Start a list

of your best qualities or greatest service accomplishments. Then keep it up to date. Write down the four greatest strengths you bring to your job and post them at your work place.

> **TIP:** When you have the inevitable bad day and are a little down in the dumps, pull out your brag sheet. It'll help put things in their proper perspective.

5. *Tell yourself, "You done good!"* Think talking to yourself is a little strange? It isn't. (Arguing with yourself, on the other hand, is a little suspect.) Good news gets better in the telling. If you're not quite ready to shout it from the housetops, at least tell yourself, verbally, with force and feeling, that you've done a good job.

> **TIP:** Be specific. Tell yourself exactly what you did well, better than you've ever done in the past. Then tell a co-worker, "You know, I just handled a really tough call and I left the customer feeling great." Or spread it around: "I watched you with that customer. She asked some pretty tough questions, but you had all the answers and sent her out of here feeling great. Nice job."

What gets rewarded gets repeated.

—Incentive and recognition axiom

30

Develop a Trademark

Customer service isn't about satisfaction. It's about dazzlement.

—Chip R. Bell

Have you noticed that there are some organizations you really enjoy doing business with? When you stop to ask yourself why, more often than not it comes down to people: certain individuals who have gone out of their way to make themselves memorable.

Those people have created a distinct identity in your eyes. They have developed a trademark way of giving service, one that sets them apart from ordinary, everyday, run-of-the-mill service providers and really "knocks your socks off." Knock Your Socks Off Service is delivered by individuals just like you who serve with distinction—and who, in doing so, become distinctive in their customers' eyes.

Establishing *Your* Trademark

Think about those individuals who have served you well. Ask your co-workers about the service people they admire the most or recall the best. What do you remember most about them? Why do they stand out from the pack? What can you learn from them that will make you even more memorable in your customers' eyes?

Now think about the service you provide. What is it about the way you do your job that makes people glad they dealt with you? Five minutes after the transaction, how would your customer describe you if asked to? What level of personal impression do you make? Could your customer pick you out of a crowd?

Try this three-step approach to discover your own trademark:

1. *Pick three.* Write down the names of the three best service people you've ever worked with (or been a customer of).
2. *Note five.* Under the names of each of your three outstanding service providers, try to list five things they do or habits they have that make them so good.
3. *Scan fifteen.* From your three names and five habits, you have a maximum of fifteen different possible trademarks. Or do you? Chances are, you'll find common elements on each of your three lists. You'll also find highly unique and individual traits. Any or all can give you a starting point for developing your own trademark.

There are many ways to establish your trademark. The distinction you choose should reflect your own personality, the wants and needs of your customers, and the nature of the service you provide. Here are five trademark basics that may help you get started.

Five Ways to Establish a Trademark

1. *Be reliable.* Doing what you say you are going to do, every time, is a terrific trademark. Reliability is basic to trust, which is the foundation for any lasting relationship. Can you earn your customer's trust? If you can, your customer will be back again and again.

2. *Call customers by name.* People love to hear their own

names. And more than once. But make sure it's the name they want to be called. Dr. Smith may not like to be called "Sally," while Mr. Ridge may want you to call him "Bill." When in doubt, start with the more formal title. Or ask what the customer prefers.

> **TIP:** Try to use the customer's name at least twice in the transaction. It's especially memorable when you incorporate it into the thank you: "Thanks, Leo. Come back real soon."

3. *Spell the customer (and the company's) name correctly.* Spelling names correctly demonstrates both common courtesy and professional care. We know a former bank president who routinely sent back invoices addressed to "XYZ Bank Lake" instead of the correct "XYZ Bank Lakeside." The difference may be small to you, but it's an important one to the customer.

> **TIP:** Be especially careful with names that sound simple, but have tricky spellings. Enlist your customer's help: "Thank you, Ms. Smith. Could I just verify the spelling: S-M-I-T-H? Or S-M-Y-T-H-E? And is that Chris with a *C* or Kris with a *K*?

4. *Recognize repeat customers.* If you have an exceptionally good memory, you may be able to recall a customer's name and details about their last service transaction. For most people, that's unrealistic. Fortunately, there are other ways to remember customers.

One way to build recognition into your service is to keep a record of each customer. Depending on your own workstyle, you may keep your notes in a computer file, an index card box, a manila file folder, or a Rolodex™. Whatever method works best, use it to note customer preferences and little personal items you want to remember—"Mr. Smith likes to be called John," or "Assistant coach for her son's soccer team," or "Always needs two-day turnaround"—as well as past experiences, problems, questions, or compliments.

TIP: Before and during an appointment, refer to your notes to refresh your memory for details. (Don't guess.) As soon afterward as possible, update them for next time.

5. *Know your products—and more.* It's not always easy to keep up to date on your own new product models and services, much less your competitor's. But customers look to you to know more than they do. You can distinguish yourself by turning questions you can't answer on the spot into opportunities to learn. If you don't know the answer, know where to find it.

The truth is that customer's really don't expect you to know everything, even though it may seem like it at times. In fact, admitting that you don't know something, but promising to find out and following up on that promise, can be just as an important trust builder.

Every job is a self-portrait of the person who did it. Autograph your work with excellence.

—From a poster in an auto repair shop

31

The Competence
Principle:

Always Be Learning

You're never off duty; you have to remember everything
you see.

—Holly Stiel
Concierge, Hyatt San Francisco

You've seen them. Maybe you've even worn one. You know,
those little tags that say TRAINEE. The ones that proclaim to all
the world, "Be patient, I'm still learning."

We often think of trainees as young, anxious to learn, full
of questions—and as people who can't wait to take off the
trainee label and finally know it all. But delivering Knock Your
Socks Off Service means having a lifelong learning mentality.
Learning your job doesn't stop when you turn in the TRAINEE
tag. In fact, it's just beginning. Like professional athletes, the
best customer service people are always in training, always
looking for ways to improve their performance, always seeking
out ways to hone their service edge.

What do you need to know? Think of lifelong learning as
a personal customer service workout program. Just as with any
form of effective cross-training, your fitness regimen should

cover several interrelated areas. There are four basics: technical skills, interpersonal skills, product and service knowledge, and customer knowledge. All are going to be critical to your success.

Technical Skills

- Do you know how to work the machines in your office: the phone (don't laugh—today's systems would surely baffle Alexander Graham Bell!), the copier, the fax machine, the cash register?
- Do you understand the purpose of and know how to complete the paperwork your company requires of you, and of your customers?
- Can you make your company's computers work for your customers?

Interpersonal Skills

- How good are your people skills? Ask your manager to listen in or observe while you work with a customer and then give you comments and suggestions for improvement. Make sure you get positive feedback, too.
- Ask a close friend to honestly critique your person-to-person manners.
- Can you anticipate how certain regular customers will react to certain situations? Do you talk about these "knowns" with fellow employees?

Product and Service Knowledge

- Do you know your own line? Your competitor's? Customers expect you to know more about the products and services you sell than they do. They also expect you to know something about the products and services your competitor sells so you can help them evaluate your line's advantages.
- Are there blind spots in your knowledge? Do you know all about cameras, or just about the auto-focus models you sell and service?

- Do you know what questions customers ask most about your products and services and how to answer them?

Customer Knowledge

- What does your customer want, need, and expect today? You can never know too much about your customer. Ask questions and show a genuine interest in the answers.
- What might they want the next time they do business with you? Always ask how you might help the customer in the future. And be aware that customers change— they're always learning too. Don't assume that it will always be business as usual.
- Do you have a file on your five best customers (your definition of "best" is the one to count), with notes on what you've learned about them?

Learning Is Systematic

Keep a "learning log"—a notebook or pad that's always near at hand in which you write down both questions and answers that will help you better define your learning goals and improve your service performance. Organize your efforts: You can't learn everything at once, so don't try. Focus your lifelong learning program on one area at a time.

For example, make Week One "Technical Skills Week," Week Two "Interpersonal Skills Week," and so on. Every time you think of a question, or learn something new, write it down in the appropriate place in your learning log.

Your workout goals might look like this:

Week One— TECHNICAL:	"I will learn how the customer invoice process works."
Week Two— INTERPERSONAL:	"I will view videotapes on phone skills and put what I learn to work."
Week Three— PRODUCTS/SERVICES:	"I will spend one evening in a competitor's store, noticing how their stock differs from our own."

Week Four—
  CUSTOMERS:

"I will ask three of my regular customers to tell me about how they use our products."

When you finish the four-week cycle, begin again with new goals for each week. Use the questions you wrote down during the first four weeks to help focus your learning in the next four.

> Anyone who stops learning is old, whether at twenty or eighty. Anyone who keeps learning stays young. The greatest thing in life is to keep your mind young.
>
> —Henry Ford

Resources

To help you with your lifelong learning, here is a list of basic resources, and some room to add your own.

At America's Service by Karl Albrecht (Dow Jones-Irwin, 1988).

Calming Upset Customers by Rebecca L. Morgan (Crisp Publications, 1989).

The Complete Guide to Customer Service by Linda Lash (John Wiley and Sons, 1989).

Contact: The First Four Minutes by Leonard Zunin, M.D., with Natalie Zunin (Ballantine Books, 1972).

Customer Connection Newsletter (Beverly Briggs Communications, 2552 Brittania Road, RR #2, Milton, Ont. S9T 2X6).

Front-line Service and *The Service Edge Newsletters* (Lakewood Publications, 50 South Ninth Street, Minneapolis, Minn. 55402).

The Future of U.S. Retailing by Robert A. Peterson (Greenwood Publishing Group, to be released August 1992).

"Helping Customers Cope With Technophobia" by Michael Ramundo (*MSM*, January 1991).

How to Get People to Do Things by Robert Conklin (Ballantine Books, 1979).

I Know It When I See It by John Guaspari (AMACOM Books 1991).

"I'm First": Your Customer's Message to You by Linda Silver man Goldzimer (Rawson Associates, 1989).

Increasing Customer Satisfaction Through Effective Corporate Complaint Handling (study conducted by Technical Assistance Research Programs [TARP], U.S. Office of Consumer Affairs, Consumer Information Center, Dept. 606R, Pueblo, Col. 81009).

In Search of Excellence by Thomas J. Peters and Robert H. Waterman, Jr. (Harper & Row, 1982).

Integrated Business Leadership Through Cross Marketing by Michael Baber (Warren H. Green, Inc., 1986).

Moments of Truth by Jan Carlzon (Ballinger Publishing Co., 1987).

Quality Customer Service by William B. Martin, Ph.D. (Crisp Publications, 1989).

Service America! Doing Business in the New Economy by Karl Albrecht and Ron Zemke (Dow Jones-Irwin, 1985).

The Service Edge: 101 Companies That Profit From Customer Care by Ron Zemke with Dick Schaaf (NAL Books, 1989).

Service Management: Principles and Practices, 2nd ed., by Dr. William Bleuel (Instrument Society of America, 1986).

Service Quality: A Profit Strategy for Financial Institutions by Leonard L. Berry, David R. Bennett, and Carter W. Brown (Dow Jones-Irwin, 1989).

Service Wisdom: Creating and Maintaining the Customer Service Edge by Ron Zemke and Chip Bell (Lakewood Books, 1989).

Stressless Selling, rev. ed., by Frances Meritt Stern and Ron Zemke (AMACOM Books, 1990).

Taking Care of Business: 101 Ways to Keep Customers Coming Back (Without Whining, Groveling or Giving Away the Store) by Dick Schaaf and Ron Zemke (Lakewood Books, 1991).

About the Authors

Kristin Anderson is research associate and project coordinator for Performance Research Associates, Inc. In addition to being a top PRA seminar leader, Kristin coordinated and co-managed the research that led to the companion book, *Managing Knock Your Socks Off Service*, to be published in 1992.

Kristin is a member of the International Customer Service Association (ICSA). Her writing on frontline service issues has appeared in *Training* magazine and *The Service Edge* newsletter. Before joining PRA, she taught speech communications at the college level and coached the University of Minnesota's Forensics Team.

Ron Zemke is a management consultant, journalist, and behavioral scientist who has become one of the best-known and most widely quoted authorities on the United States' continuing service revolution. As senior editor of *Training* magazine and editor of *The Service Edge* newsletter, he has covered the emergence and development of the global service economy. He formed Performance Research Associates, Inc., his Minneapolis-based consulting group, in 1972.

Ron has authored or co-authored ten books, including *The Service Edge: 101 Companies That Profit From Customer Care* and the best-selling *Service America! Doing Business in the New Economy.*

Dick Schaaf, president of Vernacular Engineering of Burnsville, Minnesota, served as executive editor and chief blender for the creation of *Delivering Knock Your Socks Off Service.* For his insights and yeoman's service, the authors are deeply grateful.

LILY TOMLIN

stars in an exciting new series of comedy
training films based on this book!

For preview or further information, please call

1-800-359-1935

or write to:

MENTOR MEDIA
1929 Hillhurst Avenue
Los Angeles, CA 90027
Tele: 213-667-1100
FAX: 213-667-0029